WINDOWS
OF
OPPORTUNITY

by
Sherri Cortland, N.D.

OZARK
MOUNTAIN
PUBLISHING

For permission, serialization, condensation, adaptions, or for our catalog of other publications, write to Ozark Mountain Publishing, Inc., P.O. Box 754, Huntsville, AR 72740, ATTN: Permissions Department.

Library of Congress Cataloging-in-Publication Data
Cortland, Sherri, 1957-
   Windows of Opportunity, by Sherri Cortland
Through automatic writing, the author's Guide Group provides channeled insight into the relationships and challenges that are part of our daily lives.

1. Channeling   2. Reincarnation   3. Life Plans & Purpose   4. Automatic Writing
I. Cortland, Sherri, 1957-   II. Automatic Writing   III. Metaphysics
IV. Title

Library of Congress Catalog Card Number: 2009934153

ISBN: 978-1-886940-61-1

Cover Art and Layout: www.enki3d.com
Book set in: Times New Roman, Invitation
Book Design: Julia Degan

Published by:

PO Box 754
Huntsville, AR 72740

WWW.OZARKMT.COM
Printed in the United States of America

Table of Contents

NOTES FROM THE AUTHOR

After reviewing the final draft of this book, my dear friend, Heidi Winkler, asked me if there was any dictation from the Guide Group that I didn't include in this book. The answer is yes. Intertwined in the dictation for the book were many personal messages to me from my Guides that had nothing to do with the subject matter of this book, and because of their personal nature, I did not include them here. There were also bits and pieces of dictation on subjects that were not meant to be part of this book, but will be included in the next book, "Raising Your vibrations for the New Age."

Heidi also felt very strongly that I should explain how I organized the dictation for this book. The information was not dictated in the order you see it here; the Guide Group dictated a few sentences on a given topic one day, went on to other things, and would come back to a given topic days or weeks later. When the dictation was finished, I printed out a copy of the notes, cut them up into paragraphs, and then sorted them by topic. Next, I sorted the paragraphs under each topic into an order that I hoped would make sense to the reader, and then added my "commentary." This took some time to complete as I wanted to make sure that the order made sense and the information dictated was properly placed into each chapter.

It is also very important for you to know that I don't consider myself to be an expert on automatic writing, meditation, or new age subjects. I am just a human being engaged in a personal search for truth and enlightenment, someone who wants to know why she is here living this life on this planet, and trying to make sense of the tragedy that is so very much part of every day life. That is why, wherever possible, I've given you the names of authors and books that have helped me during my personal search. There are many wonderful books available on many subjects, and I encourage you to seek out as much information as you can, find what resonates within you, and continue on your own personal search for truth and enlightenment. I started on my path many years ago, but I feel like I have only taken a couple of baby steps! I expect to be reading, listening, searching for, and implementing information until it's my turn to join the Guide Group on the other side.

CHAPTER ONE
Getting Started

I did not write this book willingly. In the following chapters you'll find some of the biggest mistakes I've made in my life, along with some of my most embarrassing moments, displayed in glorious black and white for all the world (including my family, friends, and employer!) to read. My Guide Group specifically chose these snapshots from my life to teach me and to help others recognize the "windows of opportunity" that appear in our everyday lives. My Guide Group (hereafter referred to as the "GG") was unrelenting in their desire for the personal information they gave me through automatic writing to be passed on to others who might benefit from my learning experiences. The GG wants us to understand that it's how we handle the so-called "ordinary events" that make up our daily lives that enable us to grow and progress, or keep us stagnant. They use my less than stellar moments to illustrate their points, and that is why I was not thrilled about writing this book when I first undertook the project under my GG's direction.

The information dictated by the GG is italicized, and their words are written here exactly as they were dictated to me, and interlaced between background commentary from me.

There are four reasons this book was written: (1) to help us recognize ordinary, every day experiences and situations as "windows of opportunity" for growth and learning; (2) to help us step through those windows faster, so we can learn our life lessons with the least amount of pain and drama; (3) to help us understand why bad things happen to good people, and our individual roles in making them happen, and 4) to help us wake up and take a proactive role in raising our personal vibrational level and that of the planet Earth as a whole. At 51 years old, I have had enough drama for one lifetime, so I am very happy to

1

have received this insight so I can spot my windows as quickly as possible.

Most of the dictation for this book took place in 2004, yet I didn't put the notes together until 2006, or even attempt to find a publisher until the middle of 2007. During the Summer of 2008, I got a call from Dolores Cannon, President and founder of Ozark Mountain Publishing, saying that her company would like to publish this book. At Dolores' suggestion, I expanded on some of the sections by including additional dictation from the GG that I had originally intended to put into a separate book. The GG also dictated some additional material about Atlantis, the Baby Boomer generation, and the 2008 presidential election that they wanted added to the original material. These additions were finished within a two-week period after Dolores' call to me. If I could add 30 pages in two weeks, why did take me years to put the notes together and try to find a publisher in the first place? That's an easy question to answer—because I was afraid. Afraid of what others might think. Will my family and friends think I'm crazy; will I lose my job because I take dictation from entities on the other side of the veil? Only time will tell! Among the many things I learned from the GG is that facing and overcoming fear is something I need to work on for my own personal growth, and writing this book provided the perfect window of opportunity for me to start overcoming my greatest fear—the fear of being thought of as "weird."

In 1989, my dear friend and then employer, Sunna Rasch (Founder of Periwinkle Productions, Inc.; author of the book, "*I Really Want to Feel Good About Myself*"; and writer and producer of "*Halfway There*," an award-winning drug abuse prevention play for young audiences) and I decided to take a course on psychic development from Cyndi, a well-known psychic in Monticello, New York. Sunna was well acquainted with Cyndi and had been working with her for several years. There were about 15 people in our class, and every week Cyndi gave a workshop and demonstrations about different "New Age" topics like seeing auras, contacting your guides, and past life regression. She was also a very talented medium. About 6 weeks into the class, the topic for the evening was "automatic writing," and that night my life, as they say, changed forever! As Cyndi announced that evening's subject while simultaneously handing out writing paper, I picked up my pen, held it over the paper, looked around the room and confidently proclaimed, "I've been trying to do this for months—this is *not* going to happen for me!"

As I was loudly and emphatically announcing to the class that I would never be able to do automatic writing, I suddenly felt something (or someone!) firmly grip my hand and arm. Before I knew what was happening, the pen was going around and around in a circular motion on the paper! I was staring down at my hand in shock, and my mouth was wide open! Everyone in the class was watching me and especially watching my hand. I was watching my hand too—because it wasn't like it was attached to me; it was like it had a "mind" of its own!

Cyndi rushed over and directed me to "take control." Take control!? How? Take control of what? I continued to draw circles on the paper, until, after a couple of minutes went by (it seemed like an hour at the time), I felt my arm relax and my hand and the pen stopped moving. No words were written on the paper that first night, just a lot of circles and scribbles, but the channel I had been trying for months to establish was actually opening. I was so surprised and excited! And a little scared, too. Cyndi explained to the class that automatic writing is a way for us to communicate with our guides and with our higher selves. She shared with us that we are all born with at least two guides who stay with us throughout our lives, and that others come to be with us when we need them. She told us that our "higher self" is the part of us that is connected to the Universal Consciousness, and is the part of us that is aware of why we are here, and what we need to accomplish in this lifetime.

Cyndi was very emphatic that we must always say a prayer of protection before starting an automatic writing session, or any channeling session, to keep lower level entities from attaching themselves to us. Like attracts like, and for the most part, only spirits of the highest intentions will come through, but for those occasions when others might try, you want to be sure you are protected from unwanted attention [See the chapter on Automatic Writing for instructions and the prayer of protection that Cyndi gave to Sunna and me].

During the same time period that I was taking Cyndi's psychic development course, I was also working on my B.A. in Communications at Mount St. Mary College in Newburgh, New York. Because "The Mount" is a Catholic college, students are required to take a minimum number of credits in religious studies. That year, they were offering a new class called "Meditation East and West," which I signed up for immediately.

My on-going homework assignment was to meditate for 20 minutes every day. The Sister who was teaching the course tested the class twice a week by watching us from behind while we meditated. She was watching to see if we stayed still or if we squirmed in our seats—that's how she said she could tell how much progress we were making with our practice.

So now I had two things to work on, my automatic writing and my meditation, and as I practiced each of these subjects individually, I got better at both of them. Cyndi taught us that it's best to do automatic writing at the same time every day; and my meditation teacher said that it was best to meditate at the same time each day.

On weekdays, I set aside 30 minutes every morning before leaving for work to meditate and work on my automatic writing. Weekends were a challenge as my then-husband and I had just closed on two cottages that were "handyman specials," and we devoted every weekend to working on those little houses, getting them ready to be rented. It was winter in upstate New York when all of this was taking place, and so I took a little space heater to help me stay warm, an egg timer, and a pad and pen, and went into the cottage we were not working on that day, so I could have some privacy. I would sit on the floor with my back against the wall and meditate for 20 minutes. When the timer went off, I would attempt to do automatic writing for 10 minutes. Then, I picked up my paintbrush or hammer and got back to work!

After that night at Cyndi's when my hand first starting moving around on the paper, I had no trouble at all making the connection again; in fact, I drew hundreds of circles! After about a month of that, even though I was happy to make the connection, I quickly became bored and frustrated. I wanted words! Finally, enough was enough, and I called Cyndi for advice. She told me to ask who was trying to come through, and then to ask that entity to give me a message. I did so and almost immediately, the name "Jeremy" was written on the paper. Jeremy is one of the two main guides watching over me during this lifetime.

And so I began happily writing with Jeremy at 7:00 a.m. every morning before work. As time went on, other guides and entities started "dropping in" to write with me for short periods of time, including Olexeoporath, Selena, and Charles. Each entity had specific information to share with me, and then moved on to other projects, with the exception of Jeremy. Jeremy has been with me since birth and he is the leader of the guide group that dictated the material that is the basis of this book.

The rest of the guide group includes guides who have imparted information to me through automatic writing in the past, some who are with me presently, and this really shocked me at first—some of my "deceased" family members. Oh, yes. You read that correctly. Some of my "dead" relatives are part of my GG. Do you remember me telling you earlier that one of the reasons I was publishing this book was to help me work on my fear of being labeled as "weird?" I'm pretty sure that revealing that I have relatives on the other side of the veil communicating with me through automatic writing is a big step in my coming-out party! My stomach is in knots just thinking about what my "living" relatives, friends, and my employer will think when they read this, but here goes: Joining Jeremy and the other guides for the purpose of writing this book were Marjorie Knapp (my maternal Grandmother), Linda Knapp (my cousin on my mother's side) and Gracie Dobbs (my great aunt and Marjorie Knapp's sister).

Once, my Grandpa Knapp "stopped in" to write with me, and that really took me by surprise! It was the first time a relative wrote with me, and I was very excited. I remember telling my Mother about it, and she gave me questions to ask to make sure it was really him! Mom was very much aware of my new "writing skill" and she was someone I could share it all with and not worry about being "weird." I only wrote with Grandpa Knapp two or three times, but what a great experience that was!

My grandmother was the "spokes guide" for much of this project and much of the dictation I received came to me as if I were on the computer in a chat room with her. Every morning, my sister, Kathy Seeley (who is on this side of the veil!), and I e-mail for a few minutes before going to work. She has been a constant source of encouragement for this work, and while she doesn't qualify as a "guide," she was very much a part of the daily group. What you are reading is very much a family collaboration!

As I said earlier, it has taken me this long to put the notes into a book format because of fear—I didn't want to "out" myself. Why was I so scared? Because nine years before the dictation for this booked started I had a little taste of what can happen when people find out you have "new age" beliefs. In 1995, some very nasty rumors were spread about me at work by a former friend and co-worker. She deliberately spread the rumors to keep me from being promoted, and it worked—not once, but twice! Two years later, I got a much better position than the ones I previously lost out on, but to this day I remain a little afraid of opening up on the subjects of automatic writing, reincarnation, Karma, ETs—pretty much everything that's included in this book. You would be afraid, too, if you lost two promotions because of your beliefs!

But it's time for me to "come out"—as Lou Martin* informed me while I was working on this book. Lou is a conscious channel and spiritual counselor whom I met in 2000, during a trip to Sedona, Arizona with my husband, Ted Dylewski. Ted very kindly traveled to Sedona with me so I could meditate on Bell Mountain and visit some of the energy vortexes in the area. One day, as we were exploring Sedona, we stopped into a wonderful new age shop where Lou was working, and we each had a reading. In November 2005, as I was trying to force myself to pull this book together, my personal "fear factor" was surfacing big time, so I called Lou for a reading. The first thing out of his mouth was this: "Sherri, the time has come for you to accept that you are one of the so-called 'weirdos' and get on with this project!" I hadn't even told him WHY I wanted a reading AND, this is very important—Lou doesn't really know me. I met him once in Sedona several years ago, and I've called him maybe three times over the last ten years for phone readings. For him to use the word "weirdo" blew me away.

> * Lou is now living and working in Ireland where he continues to help others find their spiritual path through "Lightheart Pleiadian Channeling." He is a conscious channel for the Pleidians, who are mentioned in Chapter 7 of this book. His website address is: http://members.Tripod.com/chaneling/index.htm

Well, as you know by now, the last thing I want is to be thought of is as a "weirdo" but after that reading, as I thought about what Lou said, I realized that I'm probably not the only one to ever worry about what other people thought about them because they were writing about new age topics. Anyway, Lou assured me that I would be in good company, and as I look back on some of the first new age books that I'd ever read, I realize that I have a lot less to lose than some of the other New Age writers!

When I first started on my personal search for the truth in the late 80's, I began with books written by Ruth Montgomery and Shirley MacLaine. Ruth Montgomery was a well-known reporter and top white house correspondent in Washington, DC, and

Shirley MacLaine was a respected actress. Why would they jeopardize their careers and reputations to write New Age books? They didn't need the money, and we all know that Shirley MacLaine is the butt of many jokes for the important information she's brought to the public over the years. I remember feeling at the time that they had so much to lose by writing books and lecturing about reincarnation, channeling, UFOs, what's on the other side of the veil, and inner transformation, that there just **had** to be something to what they were saying. I felt then, and I still feel today, that they opened themselves up to ridicule because, for so many of us, they would be considered *credible* sources for the "in"credible information they brought to us.

When I first read the Montgomery and MacLaine books, most of the information contained in them was new to me, but I've seen much of it repeated in different words in different books over the years. One of my concerns, as I started assembling the notes for this book, was that much of the information I received for this project is pretty basic. What I've been told by the GG and by several psychics to whom I turned for advice on this subject, is that while much of the information in the following chapters isn't new to me personally, it will help many people to "wake up" and move forward on their path to enlightenment. It seems to me that helping even one person start to recognize their personal windows of opportunity is worth pulling myself out of the new age closet. So after speaking with Lou, I decided to proudly put on my "weirdo" badge, sit down at the computer, and finish this book. Here is what Jeremy had to say at the start of this project as he gently coaxed me to get off my rear and get to work:

> *"Sherri, I will lead this group as I led you in the past. I will help you remember what your mission is, as you seem to have lost the zeal for this mission. You can overcome your fears. Why would we lead you down a road that would make you unhappy? All we are asking of you is to sit*

*down with us for fifteen or twenty minutes a day,
clear your mind, and let us do the rest. Even
though it may seem out of synch, there is a
method to our madness."*

My Grandmother chimed in with the following:

*"You are part of an overall mission to help bring
people to the light. To help bring an
understanding of who they are, and what they can
do to progress in a quicker way. How will you do
that? Well, you do that by just being who you are,
but you also must come out of the closet a little
more and that is where the group comes in. If you
will clear your mind, we will tell you all you need
to know to continue your mission. You can do
this. It will be as easy as walking two doors down
and plopping yourself down on the couch!"*

From the time I was eight years old until I was fifteen, my family
lived two houses down from my Grandmother. My sisters,
Debbie and Kathy, my brother Jeff and I could always be found
over at her house having tea and watching game shows on
television with Gram. I'm part of a mission that includes writing
this book—no pressure there! Writing a book will be as easy as
plopping myself down on her couch? That's Gram for you! She
continued with the following:

*"You are here to help others learn to think for
themselves and to help them find the light. You
are someone who opens doors for people and you
do that by example. Standing on a street corner
and talking about what you believe in is all well
and good, but the best way to get people to open
up and ask questions is to live what you believe.*

9

*You do a pretty good job of that with just a few
exceptions. One is road rage and another is that
your temper is short with people when they don't
do what you want them to do. You can work on
both of these things through yoga."*

I think there are worse shortcomings that could have been
highlighted here, but Gram was right about the road rage and the
temper. In case you're wondering, I now take yoga classes at the
Yogamatrix Studio in Orlando, Florida. In addition to Yoga and
Yoga Teacher Training classes, Edely Wallace also teaches
workshops on the philosophy of yoga, which helped me
overcome a very nasty case of road rage. Have you ever heard the
saying that when you are ready to learn, the right teacher will
appear? That's how it happened with Edely. I started taking
Yoga at work with my friend Kathey Condon, where they were
offering a class once a week, but the class was canceled due to
poor attendance. I found another Yoga studio, and they closed
shortly after I joined. Almost simultaneously, the Yogamatrix
Studio opened five minutes from my house, and I met Edely.
Edely began her study of Yoga in 1983, two years after a serious
road accident that took the lives of more than thirty people and
confined her to a wheel chair for several years. Unable to walk,
she dedicated the next five years of her life to an intense study of
Yoga. She eventually contradicted the medical statement that she
would never be able to walk again without support and now
teaches Yoga and Yoga-related classes and workshops. Her story
is such an inspiration to me—getting over a little road rage was
nothing compared to what Edely faced and overcame.

I'm sure that some of you are wondering how I can know that
the dictated material in this book is from the GG and not just
information that I've made up. This is something that I've
personally questioned many times since I first started doing
automatic writing back in the 80s. "Am I crazy?" is a thought
that goes through my head a lot. I've questioned myself about
it, I've questioned the guides, and I've asked experienced

psychics if I was really receiving this information from the other side. My conclusion is that if I were crazy, I probably wouldn't be asking. Whenever I receive information, I get goose bumps—over the years I have been told by various channelers and psychics, and I've read in many books, that such goose bumps are a sign of spiritual contact and spiritual acknowledgement; a way of knowing that you are truly receiving information and not making it up yourself.

I also KNOW unequivocally, and without a doubt, that the last thing I would do, if I *were* making this up, would be to include deceased family members as part of the GG. It seems to me that when my family hears who makes up the GG, they will very much question my sanity. I think most people would more easily accept other-wordly guides with names like "Olexeoporath" and "Selena," before they would accept that I'm in touch with my "Grandma Knapp"—but maybe not. We'll see.

I can tell you this much, I loved being in contact with Gram every day and it quickly became apparent to me that just because you're on the other side, you don't lose your sense of humor! As I mentioned earlier, two of my GG were sisters in this life, and they couldn't have been more different! My Grandmother, Marjorie Knapp, did not like cats at all, and my Great Aunt, Gracie Dobbs, loved them. In fact, she and her husband, Ernie, had lots of cats, and I guess she would have been considered a "cat lady" when she was alive. About eight years ago, my husband Ted and I started rescuing and "fixing" feral cats that found their way into our yard, some of whom decided to stay and live with us, and so now I guess I'm a little bit of a cat lady myself, much to the amusement of my family and friends. When I started taking dictation for this book, Aunt Gracie wrote that I should consider it a compliment when people call me by her name, because kindness to animals is a sign of a highly-developed entity. My Grandmother then chimed in that she thinks having 13 cats is a little too developed! And that is just what I would have expected Gram to say—no matter what side of the veil she might be on! Enough about me and my cats, let's get to the good stuff from the GG!

CHAPTER TWO
Karma

Here is what the group had to say about those of us currently incarnated in human bodies:

> *"We will begin with a talk of inspiration. The human being is not what it seems. Humans have tremendous capacity, which many never aspire to utilize. Why? Because for the most part, humans are unaware of the Source from whence they come. Some human beings believe in God, some do not. Human beings believe in a myriad of things, but many never reach out or search for the truth, except for a relative handful out of the countless millions who decide to take up the quest.*
>
> *Why is it this way? To begin with, through the centuries, human beings have re-written or altered everything handed down to them. This was done to gain power, to make the information fit their personal and/or political agendas and to give them a hold over others, or as a way to sway others to their own agenda. It's all about power; and by manipulating and purposely re-interpreting religious documents, human beings find ways to accomplish their goals by removing those who oppose them."*

To hear from the group that religions were altered for political purposes wasn't really a surprise to me. Many books talk about Constantine of Rome and how he copied pagan religious practices and incorporated them into early Christianity. He purposely absorbed pagan holidays and ideas into his new church to make it more palatable for the masses. Next, Constantine set out to obliterate the very pagan religious practices he had copied in his quest to unite Rome under one religion, Christianity, which he could then use to control his subjects. Among the pagan practices that Constantine incorporated into Christianity were the trinity and many religious holidays and feasts. My family is Catholic. When I was married to my first husband, Bruce, I started attending church services with his family on Wednesday nights and Sunday mornings—they belonged to a Baptist Church in Montgomery, New York. I didn't feel like I was turning my back on Catholicism or on my family—my feeling has always been that there is one God, one Creator, so what does it matter what church you go to on Sunday?

Switching churches turned out to be an important part of my spiritual development—it's what made me break away from formal religion. One Sunday morning back in 1980, the Pastor's sermon revealed that "those who have statues of Christ or the Virgin Mary were practicing idolatry and would not be going to heaven." My entire family is Catholic! Some wore crosses with Jesus on them! I owned crosses with Jesus on them! I waited until after the service and asked the Pastor to go over this with me again, I really wanted to make sure I was getting this straight. So I asked him, "Are you saying that anyone who wears a cross with Jesus on it or who has a statue of the Virgin Mary will go to hell?" I just couldn't wrap my head around the idea that me, or anyone in my family, would be forced to suffer eternal damnation because of our jewelry and statuary choices.

That Pastor stood by what he preached. That was one step out the door for me, but I continued to go to church. Step two towards the door came just a couple of weeks later during a service about how believing in the Theory of Evolution was evil, Darwin was evil, and that dinosaur bones were planted by Satan to throw us off the path! And a few weeks later, when he preached a sermon about gays and lesbians going to hell, I was out the door. What kind of God would condemn people for being different? What kind of God would send people to hell for having a statue or wearing the "wrong" cross? And can you picture a Johnny-Appleseed Satan, running around the Earth planting pseudo-dinosaur bones to lead us down the path of eternal damnation? Please!

The group continued with a statement about Karma and our capacity for good and evil:

> *"People have a tremendous capacity for good and a tremendous capacity for 'evil.' Which way will they turn? Well, it's a matter of Karma and what they want to accomplish, because the bottom line is that there really is no such thing as 'evil.'"*

And then they left me hanging until the next day! Fortunately they took up right where they left off.

Intro to Karma

> *"There is a force working within the universe —some would call it 'evil.' It is nothing more than the law of cause and effect. It is Karma. Karma can be a positive experience or it can be a difficult experience. It depends on what you've planned for yourself to learn in this lifetime."*

My personal understanding of Karma is that it is a Universal Law based on action and reaction, kind of a cause and effect where if we do something against another person or against nature, we will have to pay the piper for it during our current incarnation (instant Karma) or during a future lifetime. It's also my understanding that if we do nice things, good things will come to us, during this lifetime, or in another. It's kind of a "you reap what you sow" type of law.

15

In his book, *Universal Law for the Aquarian Age*, Dr. Frank Alper says that Universal Law is an expanding and contracting vibration that is always in motion. As Dr. Alper explains in his book, "If, after an action is taken, an error has been made, it can be corrected by another action called Karma. This [law] constitutes the growth of mankind….[Karma] is established not so much as a restrictive measure, as it is a *guideline* to assist one in the selection of a proper path, and to help one avoid error in the pursuit of one's life."

My personal studies have led to me to believe that Karma is very much a part of our every day lives, and so I am fascinated by a popular TV show called "My Name is Earl." It's a show about Karma, where the main character, Earl, realizes that the bad luck he experiences is attributable to the bad things he's done to others. He's made a list of all the bad things he's done and each week he sets out to make things right for one of the people on his list!

Karma is as important to the material in this book as it is to Earl; in fact, Karma is the foundation for most of the channeled information from the GG, and they continued with their discussion of Karma with the following insights:

> "*There is a force working within the universe called Karma. It is the law of cause and effect. It is the energy that you send forth whether positive or negative and it is the energy that you receive back either positive or negative.*
>
> *Karma can be a positive experience or it can be a difficult experience. It depends on what you've planned for yourself to learn in each lifetime.*
>
> *Cause and effect is a pretty simple concept. Any action will have a reaction. That's pretty simple, yes? Well, the difficult part comes when you have to find imaginative ways in each lifetime*

to accept payback from others whom you have hurt or damaged OR even to bestow positive payback on people who have helped you.

And so it is very important for people to quickly figure out what they are here for if they want to move ahead. The less time they waste figuring it out and the more time they spend doing it, the sooner their work will be done and they can enjoy the rest of their lives.

Everything must balance in the end so if you've sent forth negative energy, you will receive back negative energy. If you send out positive energy, you will receive back positive energy. There comes a time in the lives of many a lightworker where they don't have to deal with the Karmic experience anymore.

Negative and positive energy can be sent forth with thoughts, not just with actions. To wish well for people and to wish health and forgiveness for people will bring positive energy back to you. To wish ill for people will only bring the same back to you."

One of the most important things that I took away from this section personally is that we must take responsibility for our thoughts as well as our actions, and we must train ourselves to watch our thoughts just as we watch what comes out of our mouths. Taking responsibility for our thoughts and words will help us bring more light to the planet and help us raise our own vibrational levels. The GG will have more to say about our thoughts in the next section.

Planning your life takes on new meaning!

> *"There are groups of souls/entities with whom we
> tend to travel [incarnate], but change roles within
> our soul/entity group. Sometimes a particular
> soul/entity is our friend during one incarnation,
> and a spouse or sibling in others. We change
> roles depending on what is necessary for the
> growth of the central soul/entity for whom the
> planning is being done."*

This is how the GG introduced the subject of how we plan our
incarnations. This subject wasn't new to me, and most of what
I know about planning sessions for our various incarnations I
learned from the Kryon writings channeled by Lee Carrol. I've
read all the Kryon books and I was privileged to attend a Kryon
channeling session when Lee Carrol came to Orlando. I highly
recommend the Kryon series to anyone who wants in-depth
knowledge about how we set up and plan each one of our
lifetimes. Kryon also provides a wealth of information about
reincarnation, the current shifting of the vibrational level of our
planet, and what that means to the evolution of the human race.

At this point, the GG asked that I elaborate on planning
sessions so you will better understand what they mean when they
say:

> *"Karma can be a positive experience or it can be
> a difficult experience. It depends on what you've
> planned for yourself to learn in each lifetime."*

The first thing to know is that we have the responsibility and the
power to plan every one of our incarnations. Picture yourself
sitting at a conference table with many other entities. You've
known these entities for literally eons, and spent many different
lifetimes with them in different capacities. Some of them are
beloved teachers and guides who are part of the meeting to advise

you and make sure that you are not being overly optimistic with what you think you can accomplish during the incarnation you are planning. All of the entities present know you. They love you. They know your strengths and they know your limitations.

You have a "laundry list" of things you want to accomplish during your next incarnation; this list includes debts you need or want to repay (Karma) and other experiences you wish to have for the growth of your soul. Based on what you want to accomplish during this next lifetime, you choose your parents by searching for a familial situation that will provide you with the best opportunities to accomplish the items on your list. Your next set of parents are probably sitting right there at that conference table with you! And so are other members of what will be your new family, along with the friends and acquaintances you will make, and even your future "enemies."

Like an outline for a book complete with chapters, you and your planning committee will create a lifetime of opportunities for you to accomplish the things YOU want to accomplish! You will even create back-up opportunities in case you don't get it quite right the first time you try. These opportunities for learning and growth are called **"windows of opportunity,"** and learning to spot them and take advantage of them will be covered in depth later in this book. The important thing to comprehend right now is that each and every one of us decides *before* we are born exactly what we plan to learn and experience.

Now back to Karma. Karma is a way for us to rectify situations that we have been involved in that somehow created negative energy. It is also a way for us to receive positive energy *from* others, and transfer positive energy *to* others. This seems pretty simple and straightforward, but it can become very complicated:

> *"Negative and positive energy can be sent forth*
> *with thoughts, not just with actions. To wish well*
> *for people and to wish health and forgiveness for*

19

people is a positive cog in the Karmic wheel, and it will bring positive energy back to you. To wish ill for others will only bring the same back to you. Something many people don't realize is that thoughts are extremely powerful things and they do impact your life and the lives of those around you.

How can we tell you how important this is? As the energy of the planet changes and we come into the new age in a more aggressive way, there will eventually be more new energy than old energy. As people become more enlightened, their energy shifts to a higher vibration, and so is the Earth shifting to a higher vibration. As these changes continue to occur, for they are ongoing, thoughts will become even more powerful. And so it is that the human population must become aware of their power. The things they 'think' will in time come into being, and the further into the new age we move, the sooner those thoughts will manifest. That is the good and bad, the yin and yang of it.

Everyone must watch their words, they must choose what they say as wisely as they choose their actions because their thoughts, whether positive or negative, WILL come firing back at them like silver bullets from the Lone Ranger! Tell everyone they must take care when it comes to their thoughts!"

Whew! Watching what we say is one thing—it's not that difficult to edit the words that come out of our mouths, especially when you know the effect your words will have on this and future life times. But policing your *thoughts*? Thoughts are things? At first glance, that seems impossible. But if you think about it,

20

everything that's ever been invented or built or is put into place had to first be a thought or idea in someone's mind; so generating positive or negative energy with our thoughts isn't that far-fetched. But how many different thoughts do we have every day and about how many different subjects? In my Yoga class, when the mind is jumping around from one subject to another, we call it "monkey brain," and I have monkey brain a lot. When I first received this section, the thought of scrutinizing my thoughts seemed impossible to me. But over time, I've trained myself to become more aware of my thoughts as they were forming, and I'm working hard to be much more careful about what I put out into the universe. It's not easy, but based on what the GG said above, it's something that we need to start focusing on as a way to grow, and to lower the amount of negativity that we put out into the atmosphere.

Accelerated Karma

Karmic debt that is incurred and paid for in a short span of time within the same incarnation (lifetime) is called "accelerated" or "instant" Karma:

> *"Not everyone who is incarnated at the present time is here because they have a debt to work off. There are those who are incarnated who do not have to deal with the Karmic cycle any longer. This is because they have pushed past that and were forgiven any past Karma that needed to be worked out. However, they must be careful of creating new Karmic debts to be paid during this life or later lifetimes. That is why you see so much Instant Karma taking place. Many entities are here in their last incarnation and they must pay the piper, so to speak, immediately. Which means in a day, a minute, a week or a year! It is that fast on the accelerated lifetime plan! Those*

Karmic debts are paid quickly so the entities can finish one project and move on to the next. It is really impossible to be incarnated and not incur Karmic debt. It is very hard to live that way, so there is usually some that must be paid along the way and that is just the way it is."

The first time I heard John Lennon's song, "Instant Karma," I got chills; and I still get them when I hear it played today on our local oldie's radio station. Look at these lyrics and see what you think:

"Instant Karma's gonna get you,
Gonna look you right in the face,
Better get yourself together darlin',
Join the human race,
How in the world you gonna see,
Laughin' at fools like me,
Who on earth d'you think you are,
A superstar, Well, right you are.
Instant Karma's gonna get you;
Gonna knock you off your feet;
Better recognize your brothers;
Ev'ryone you meet..."

I think John Lennon understood Karma! And the more I've learned about Karma, the more I've come to understand what John Lennon was writing about in this song. We are all interconnected to each other. We impact each other with our words and actions, and there are consequences for our words and actions. I think one of the most important steps I've taken on my spiritual path thus far is to realize how crucial words and actions are to our personal growth as spiritual entities. And this is one of the reasons the GG keeps reminding me to work on my road rage and temper challenges—words spoken in anger not only hurt other people, but they also incur Karmic debt for the speaker.

If keeping my mouth shut will help me reduce the number of future incarnations I'll have to spend working out Karmic debt[1], then I will learn to keep my big mouth shut! I've been working on this for a couple of years, and while I do backslide occasionally, I know that I'm becoming more and more mindful when it comes to realizing the Karmic impact of the things I say and do and think. I know I still have a lot of work to do, particularly in my everyday interactions with other people. I think a big part of my challenge is that I want the best for my friends, family, and co-workers. I want them to succeed so much, I have a tendency to judge and criticize them when they don't do what I think they should be doing! I clearly see the potential in those around me and I want them to attain the level of success they deserve. But I've come to realize that in doing this, I'm not thinking about their carefully thought-out life plan; I'm trying to make them conform to my ideal of where they should be now and where they should be going in their lives. I know now that this behavior is tantamount to interfering with another's freewill. Unless of course, I'm asked my opinion. Which I will happily give!

As I was becoming more aware of this behavior, I began to notice that I was much less understanding and much more vocal about the mistakes and shortcomings (I should really say **"what I *perceive* as the mistakes"**) of those who are the closest to me. Recognizing this behavior was step one. Now I am in the process of re-training myself, and sometimes it's still hard for me to keep my mouth shut, even though I know that judging others is absolutely wrong, and that I will incur Karmic debt because of it. Karma is a simple concept to understand, but not so easy to avoid. And as the GG keep reminding me, recognizing what we're each here to work on is very important, and it's how we

---

* For a comprehensive study of life planning sessions and accelerating the payment of Karmic debt, please read "Kryon Book One: The End Times," and "Kryon Book Two: Don't Think Like a Human."

work on our projects that will make the difference in our spiritual growth—which I think, is their nice way of encouraging me as I realize how much work I have ahead of me! The GG asked me to end this section with the following:

> *"Here's one way to look at it: Some people pay off their credit card bills in one lump sum payment, others pay them off in smaller, easier payments. Some people pay off their credit cards and stop using them; while others pay them off, charge some more, and pay them off again. During our pre-incarnation planning sessions we decide what life debts we're going to pay, and how we're going to pay them. Then we create many windows of opportunity to help us make those payments. Paying off our Karmic debt and trying not to incur more debt takes up a lot of our time as human beings!"*

When Bad Things Happen To Good People

According to the GG, "bad" things don't just happen to us, we plan them:

> *"Sometimes there are lessons to be learned that require harsh circumstances. Sometimes it's necessary to experience the death of a loved one or a sickness that is prolonged where we have to take care of that loved one in order to learn and grow. The entity that dies or is sick is really helping us out of love by being sick, or by being the one who comes into this life to die so we can experience what we need to experience. We have to be very careful when labeling people as villains, or as 'evil.' We should look instead at*

24

the big picture by looking for script-like occurrences, and evaluating what's happening with individual situations to see if there is a window of opportunity. If there is, and we go for it, we will accelerate learning. As we start to do this, we will gain experience in doing so. This means we will work less hard when it comes to our lessons because we will recognize them earlier.

There are Karmic debts to be taken care of, and there are growth experiences to be had. Meaning that not everything that happens is Karmic, but is planned by the individual soul to help him progress. It could be that the soul is seeking a faster progression and has chosen to undergo a very tumultuous life.

You see, we are in control of our spiritual growth—no one else. Although we each do have a group of guides and advisors who work with us to make sure that we don't take on too much in any one lifetime, we have freewill.

You've heard the saying that God doesn't give us more than we can handle? Well, it isn't God who's doing this; it's our guides, advisors and us. God is not involved in the day-to-day spiritual development of each and every soul. We have freewill that we exercise continually.

Even when bad things seem to happen, and it's incomprehensible that they should happen, there is most likely a plan behind it.

There are times when unplanned events do happen and they cause the Karmic wheel to begin to roll anew, and the entity that caused the pain will surely get it back; if not in this lifetime, then most assuredly in another. That is why it's better

> *to watch how you treat people and watch the*
> *things you do and say because most of us are not*
> *fully awake and we don't know which things we*
> *have planned and which things are incurring new*
> *Karma for us. This is part of the process of being*
> *human. We are asleep, we try to wake up and we*
> *try to make progress. Progress is so much easier*
> *to make when one is aware of how one's actions*
> *will draw consequences."*

I mentioned earlier that in the past, I've been known to have a little temper. I had a chance to go through a window of opportunity that was open so wide and was so obvious (in retrospect), that I can't believe I missed it. And honestly, I'm so ashamed of my behavior I can barely type these words. My husband, Ted, and I were flying home from our trip to Sedona, Arizona. We'd just spent a week meditating on Bell Mountain, and hiking to the energy vortexes—I was feeling very calm, very peaceful and very new agey on the trip home.

When the plane landed in Orlando, and all the passengers were standing up in the aisle waiting for the door to open so we could deplane, the woman behind me kept pushing her suitcase into me. It hurt. She did it once, and I said nothing. She did it twice and I said nothing. The third time, I turned around and nicely said, "Ma'am, I'm sure you don't realize it, but you're hitting me with your suitcase." She replied, "Too bad!" and rammed her suitcase into me again—and this time there was no doubt that it was on purpose! Well, so much for any spiritual growth from that trip—I gave her a little push back with my suitcase. I had never done anything like that in my life before or since! I'm a peaceful person, and while this was happening, I felt like I was in a play—it didn't feel real. Thank goodness it stopped there—we didn't knock each other down or anything. She was kind of shocked that I wasn't allowing her to bully me, and I couldn't believe what I did. Looking back at it now, I can clearly see that great big window—and it should have been so easy for me to go through it after a week of soaking up all that great Sedona energy. I blew that opportunity big time and you know, and I know, that I'll be paying for it in this lifetime or the next.

Acquiring "Good" Karma

Is there a way to "buy" ourselves some good Karma to balance against the bad? Is it possible to cause hurt to someone and then make donations to charities or do volunteer work to help us lessen our Karmic load?

> *"So what of doing charitable works to bank good Karma—does it earn you brownie points of any kind? Can you store up good works and subtract your Karmic debt? The answer is that it is your intention for doing something that is important. It's possible to do good things for the wrong reasons, and others will benefit from your actions—you're not hurting others by doing good things for the wrong reasons—but YOU won't be fooled. When you review the movie of your life, you'll know what your purpose was. Are you going to acquire Karmic debt because you did something nice with an ulterior motive—probably not, but you're not going to create an account of good Karma to draw from, either.*
>
> *Sending out good thoughts, thoughts of healing, prayers, and best wishes to and for people, AND MEANING what you think and send, that kind of positive energy will be returned to you. Lending a hand and volunteering because you sincerely want to help others in need, that kind of positive energy will be returned to you."*

Life Scripts

Waking up is all about understanding who we are spiritually and then claiming our power. These things don't always happen simultaneously—you can wake up spiritually and start your quest for the truth *without* claiming your power. That's what happened to me. I woke up in the 80's but it took me until 1997 to totally claim my power, and it took an extremely volatile relationship with a man I was engaged to for a short period of time to literally shake me into claiming that power.

I'd heard the term "life script" before the GG started dictating notes about it, but *never, in my wildest imagination,* did I ever think it could be applied to my own life! I learned differently from the GG! You will see my Grandmother's influence on the group as the GG pulls no punches when it comes to "telling it like it is." For the purpose of privacy (not mine, obviously!), I've changed some names.

> *"Progress is so much easier when one is aware of how one's actions will draw consequences...do you understand where we're going with this? You saw it yourself with Jim, in particular, but it was the same in all of your romantic relationships. We will tell you this too, little girl, you didn't have to have the hardships that came with that whole Jim thing. You could have learned that lesson earlier and easier. You had many chances to do so in other relationships, particularly with Joe* [my second husband] *but you chose to close your eyes and not recognize a life script when you saw one. But because you chose to learn certain lessons in this lifetime in order to move forward, you set yourself up with a back up plan that really knocked the sense into you.*

*And that is what people do—they have many
windows of opportunity to learn the same thing.
The so called "life scripts" we hear about are
fail-safes, if you will, that enable us to make sure
we learn what we came to learn; and again, so
that we can progress."*

I definitely understood where the group was going with this. My relationship with Jim, my ex-fiancé, was not particularly long, but it impacted me deeply on several levels. It was the worst relationship I was ever involved in and it brought me to new lows in my life. Ultimately, though, it did make me stand up and claim my power, and it taught me to never, ever give away that power to another person.

As the notes for this book were dictated, I was forced to review my first two marriages in light of the channeled information I received. As I looked back on those relationships, it became crystal clear (hindsight is always 20/20!) that I had two distinct windows of opportunity to learn to stand up for myself and take my power before Jim. With Jim, it was a situation where I had no choice but to take my power back or I would have sacrificed the core of my being. I believe I was firmly on the path to becoming a battered woman! The telltale signs (again hindsight is 20/20) began with escalating verbal abuse, and continued with his attempts to segregate me from my friends and family. I did not take back my power in a quiet and spiritual way; it happened during a horrible fight where Jim pushed me against the wall and actually spit in my face! I ended up **exploding** into my power.
 I remember the total shock I felt when he did that, and I also remember thinking to myself, "What do I do now? What is the protocol in a situation like this?" What I was experiencing was so foreign to me and I had no idea how to react.
  I dialed 911 as Jim pulled the phone out of the wall; the police came a few minutes later, and he moved out that night. While writing these words now, more than a decade later, I am

physically sick to my stomach to think that I ever let anyone treat me badly, or even try to keep me away from my family and friends. I can recall making excuses for him for the terrible things he said and did. Such classic, classic, signs of battering—and oh, so clear to me now, but I didn't recognize it while it was happening.

As I reflect back on it all now, I can see distinct similarities in my relationships that were not apparent to me when I was in them. At the start of each relationship, I was sure each man was completely different than the last, but in retrospect they really weren't all that different. In fact, I think they were like different levels on a video game! After much counseling from the GG, I'm pretty sure that I co-created the same basic circumstances in not two, but three different settings, with each relationship more dramatic than the previous one.

> *"Your second husband seemed different from the first, but yet was the same! They took control first in small ways, then in bigger ways, and you allowed them to do it. You rebelled at certain things: you didn't speak for a day, but you still allowed it to continue because you never stood up to them. Until, at the very end, when you stood up and left. You left Bruce, you left Joe, and then on to Jim. He was the great big window of opportunity that you hoped you would never have to use, but use it you did. Even though we tried to talk you out of it because you could have learned the lesson with Joe and still moved on to a better relationship. But you elected to leave Joe, and Jim really let you have it. You took it for a while and then you just stopped taking it. You finally woke up and found your power.*

And it's a good thing you learned it because you still had another window lined up and it would have been even worse!"

I'm guessing here, but as I was sitting at the planning table, I bet I was sure I would recognize the first window of opportunity that opened, and never have to deal with the others!

It's very clear now that in the past I would leave rather than take a stand. Had I learned to confront situations and stand up for myself early on, I would have made things much easier on myself. My first husband did things like telling me not to buy Wonder Bread—I don't even remember what he had against Wonder Bread, but I know it became a joke in my family about not buying Wonder Bread. My first marriage had problems, but looking back, I can see the windows, and they were gentle windows! But I wasn't awake enough to see them. Again, too bad for me, because I would have saved myself a lot of pain.

With my second husband, there was the proverbial "straw that broke the camel's back,' and when that happened, I was just over it. I felt like I had become low priority in his life, and I tried to approach him about it. He didn't understand how I was feeling, or maybe he just chose to ignore how I was feeling, it's hard to say. After awhile, I felt he wasn't able to, or simply wasn't going to make any changes. I dreaded telling my family about ending that marriage because I thought they were all madly in love with him and would be upset with me for leaving him. I got a big surprise when almost everyone in my family told me that they didn't like him at all and they were glad I ended it. After the divorce, they told me they didn't like the way he spoke to me, and they felt he acted like he was superior to me—things I never even noticed—I guess I still wasn't awake enough. They also told me about some nasty things they overheard him saying about different members of my family—and he said them at my Mother's house, within everyone's hearing! I was truly taken back by all of this, and I had a hard time believing it. I confronted Joe, and he admitted saying these awful things, and to top it off, he said he wasn't sorry for saying them! Even though I had already left him when I confronted him about all of this, we were going out to dinner and talking more than we had during the last three years of our marriage. I never told anyone this, but I considered giving the marriage one more try—but when he confirmed the things he said and wasn't sorry he said them, I stopped considering a reconciliation.

Joe was hardly ever around during the last couple of years of our marriage—he was very busy playing golf, tennis and pool with his friends. Because I felt so neglected, I never let on that I was planning to leave and he didn't know until the day I left. I have always regretted the way I left that marriage. As the GG have told me, I should have taken my stand while in the marriage, instead of just walking away. That would have been taking my power. But I didn't do it. It didn't even occur to me. As the group says, I could have spared myself a lot of heartache if I had. But freewill is freewill, and at the time, I didn't realize I was operating on a life script, and I didn't know what I was supposed to be working on in this incarnation. Wouldn't it be great if we could send a memo to ourselves with our "To Do" list all written out?

The scariest part of this dictation was learning from the GG that I had *another* window of opportunity set up and ready to go that would have been even *worse* than the relationship with Jim. I don't even want to think about what that might have been. I guess I really wanted to make sure that I took control of my life and claimed my power during this incarnation!

> *"Each step, each window is more difficult, until you get the message, do you see? But you did get it and you moved on to a much better relationship! No one will ever take control of you again—you control yourself. And so you see how this goes."*

Each of the three relationships the Group chose to highlight above was progressively more difficult, and more "in my face," so that I would eventually *get* the message and *learn* the lesson. After two decades of following my personal life script, I finally walked through a window of opportunity, opened up to my power, and was free to move on to other lessons and experiences, *and* to meet Ted! Here is a piece of advice from the GG:

> *"Learn the lesson on the first floor of the building instead of traveling all the way to the penthouse. The lower the floor, the easier the lesson is learned."*

Karma and the Progress of the Human Race

> *"Karma and the Karmic Wheel, how does it relate to the progress of the human race? For awhile it seemed that humans would be able to get around the terrible business of Iraq, but they were unable to avoid it, even though millions of souls did their best to send love and light to that area of the world. Those who are at the root cause of it are working through their Karma, as are the countries that opposed them.*
>
> *There is a lot of Karma built up between cultures too, not just between individuals. Sometimes countries and the people who live in them and run them will take advantage of other countries. That is the case in the Middle East. Some countries are run by rulers who take and take from the land and their people, and then don't share the wealth. In turn, the people take out their frustration on the very countries who make their rulers wealthy. The rulers have a lot to do with this because they will make the*

customer countries out to be capitalist criminals. Do you get what we are saying here? The bottom line is that the war could have been avoided. The United States is seen as a brutal force that enforces its wants and desires and politics on all people. Once Bush is out of office, the world will settle down.

As we continue to enter the new age, there will continue to be a shift in consciousness for all human beings. Some will and are making the transition easily as they have been waiting for the transition and expecting it. Others will and are having a more difficult time, because they have been so caught up in the negative energy of this century. Many won't know how to not feel angry or sad all the time. Many won't want to give up feeling angry or sad. It will be a difficult adjustment for many entities incarnated during the transition. Some will not be able to handle it all and those poor souls will commit suicide—and not necessarily the way you might envision this happening. Many entities will drink, drug and smoke themselves to death. Some will attract terminal diseases. This is sad, but part of the overall plan because the planet must shift and the new age must come into its own. That is the way with evolution."

When this was first dictated, I didn't think much about it. But in the last two years, I've seen a remarkable number of people whom I love contract, suffer and/or die from cancer. So many of my friends and acquaintances have also had many people close to them diagnosed with cancer. I can count at least 12 people that I know who are dealing with cancer right now. It can't be a coincidence. And I have several friends and family members who simply refuse to stop smoking—why? They know it's bad for them, but they continue to do it. My Mother died in the Summer of 2008 after a 16-month struggle with lung and brain cancer. She smoked through all the chemo and radiation. In the end, she could barely get out of bed, but she could still hold that cigarette. She would not stop smoking even though she knew it was hurting her chances of recovery. Maybe she just felt it was time to leave, it's hard to say from this side of the veil, but after re-reading what the GG dictated above, it seems like that might be the case.

Evolving into higher beings is what this planet has always been about, from the time that souls first entered primates and others animals to learn what a corporeal body felt like, to the very slow evolution of the ape into man as he stands today. Things have been tried, tested, learned, and this life form, the human being, is ready to cross into another evolutionary plane—the plane of higher consciousness where mankind will become aware of his affect on the planet, the ecology and the lives of people outside of his own family, workplace, city, and country.

This shift is a gradual thing and has in fact been happening for many years now. It will continue until it is fully complete. As the Indigo, Crystal, and Rainbow children grow up, they will give birth to the next evolution of entities that will populate the planet. One day, the Indigos and Crystals will replace the baby boomers, and it is their children who will really make progress by bringing peace to the planet."

Doreen Virtue has written two wonderful books about the Indigos and Crystals (*"The Care and Feeding of Indigo Children"* and

"The Crystal Children"), and there are in depth explanations of who these children are on her website: *www.angeltherapy.com.* The children of the Crystals, by the way, are called the "Rainbow" children.

> *Drugging children is a sad, sad thing that is going on today and is a response by old energy to new energy. Parents do not understand that their children are different. They do not like justifying themselves to children and that is the way with Indigos! They want to know the why behind any actions they are asked to take. They will survive this mass drugging and come into their own. It is always darkest before the dawn."*

Referring to the use of mind-altering drugs like Ritalin being given to children to make them behave better, the GG asked me to make sure to tell the parents of "difficult" children to try talking to their children and explaining to them *why* they are asking them to do something; i.e., chores or even why they need to "be quiet" at certain times. The GG suggests that we try different ways of communicating with these kids rather than resorting to drugs.

Karma: Some things to think about

- Karma is a Universal Law based on action and reaction. It is the positive or negative energy you send forth, and it is the positive or negative energy that you receive back.

- We choose our parents and plan our lives before we incarnate, including what Karmic debt we intend to pay and the experiences we need to learn in order to grow.

- We insert many "windows of opportunity" into our lives to make sure that we learn the lessons we planned for ourselves so we can grow and evolve. Learning to recognize our windows quickly will save us time and pain. Recognizing life scripts will help us wake up, take action, and go through a window.

- Thoughts are things and it's as important to watch what we think as it is to watch what we say and do.

- The more positive energy we send out into the world, the more light we draw to the planet and to ourselves, thus raising our own vibrations and those of the planet as a whole.

- We are here on this planet to learn and evolve.

CHAPTER THREE
Reincarnation

Unlimited opportunities for growth

The GG wants us to know that we have unlimited opportunities to "get it right" through reincarnation, and that each incarnation or lifetime holds many, many individual windows of opportunity for growth.

"We want to further discuss relationships and what they really mean. So many people think that this life is their one shot at happiness. What they don't realize is that it's just one part of a many-pieced puzzle wherein they learn specific lessons that will enable them to continue on in their path of spiritual growth.

If only they would understand the cycle of reincarnation and the path that takes one on, they would be so much happier. Why? Because they would recognize earlier the life scripts that keep them in the cycle of Karma, and the windows of opportunity that will get them out of that cycle. They would recognize that a particular situation is something they are here to work on, and they would hopefully take the steps through those windows much sooner to learn a particular lesson. Do you know what we mean?

The circles of life that we keep ourselves twirling around in: if we understood about reincarnation, we would recognize when we are anchored into a life script and we would plan our way out of it. But if we believe that this is our one and only lifetime, and we believe that this life is

nothing but circumstances and coincidences that
we have no control over, then what can be done?
You will live through the same situation over and
over again. But if you see it for what it is, and
you take control, your growth occurs faster and
you move on faster.
  Remember, my dear, that there is no death.
Life is merely a continuous string of
experiences—as a man, as a woman, as a person
of color, as a Caucasian. We try on different
'costumes' so that we can experience different
things, either because we want those experiences
for the fun or educational benefits it will bring us,
or because we must do it for some Karmic-
fulfillment reason, or because it will help us move
ahead faster in our schooling. For so many
entities incarnated on Earth, the Earth is a
classroom—a gigantic, round, blue and green
schoolhouse whose students will experience much
upheaval as the planet moves into the millennium
and the cleansing continues."

My Mother, Marge Ihburg, had a collection of "new age" books, although I'm not sure they were called "new age" back then—they were probably categorized as "occult." I started reading Mom's books on reincarnation when I was in my early teens, starting with her copy of Hans Holzer's *Born Again—the Truth about Reincarnation.* That book now sits on my bookshelf. Also in my library is my Grandmother's copy of Holzer's *Life After Death—the Challenge and the Evidence.* I'm not sure how I ended up with it, but I know it belonged to Gram because her name is written on the inside cover. She and my Grandfather read so many books that they would inscribe the inside covers with their signature or initials to keep track of which ones they'd already read! *Life Beyond Death* by Arthur Ford and *The Betty*

Book by Stewart Edward White, once part of my Mom's cache of new age books, at some point also took up residence in my personal library. These books were written early in the 20th century and were no doubt considered quite "out there" when they were first published. They seem pretty basic when I re-read them now, but they were and are a great place to start learning about reincarnation. Those authors were the pioneers who paved the way for Ruth Montgomery and Shirley MacLaine!

Group Karma & Reincarnation

In July 2008, the GG discussed the upcoming presidential election quite a bit. They were very excited about the history that was being made by Hillary Clinton and Barack Obama, and gave me several pages of dictation about group Karma and Atlantis, that included Al Gore, George W. Bush, and Barack Obama!

"Karma gives us the opportunity to learn from past mistakes and to grow. Reincarnation is the vehicle that allows us to put Karma into action. Today we will talk about Atlantis and the people who lived and died there. Now is the time that many Atlanteans have reincarnated together to work through their group Karma.

The people of Atlantis were a culture advanced in science and technology. They were also arrogant and geocentric, and these traits led them to self-destruction. The rise and fall of Atlantis is discussed in many books and we have nothing new to add to the history of Atlantis, but for the purpose of understanding group Karma and Reincarnation, we will discuss Atlantis now.

The United States of America is basically Atlantis reborn, as there are so many Atlantean souls currently incarnated there to fulfill a group Karmic debt and to heal themselves from the terrible destruction they caused to this planet. The destruction they caused and the damage they did to an entire continent and to the planet Earth was so great that those responsible agreed to reincarnate together and 'get it right' this time.

The time of the Atlanteans' rebirth has brought many technological achievements, including some of your favorites, Sherri, like the microwave, cell phone, and GPS. But that is not why they are here. They want to see if they can develop and succeed without being arrogant, egocentric, and causing great damage to the world. We will tell you now that both Al Gore and George W. Bush were Atlanteans, and it is no accident that they ran against each other for President. Whomever was elected would indicate the progress of the Atlanteans during this group incarnation. That election was a sort of 'temperature taking' to check on their progress as a group. Depending on which votes you count, both Gore and Bush were elected President, so close was the split between the two Baby Boomer Atlantean factions. Bush took control, and it is interesting to note here that when Bush was in Atlantis, he was directly responsible for the deterioration of relations with other continents. One of his goals for this lifetime was to lead without creating havoc and destruction. Al Gore was a chief advisor in Atlantis and he tried to stop the destruction from happening. Had he become president instead of Bush, the United States would have had a much more peaceful 8 years, but the Atlanteans had not quite learned their lesson, as indicated by the outcome of that presidential race.

The incarnated Baby Boomer Atlanteans stood divided behind both, but Bush won, not once but twice. Relationships with other countries were damaged by his "If you're not with me, you're against me" philosophy. Each presidential election was a window of opportunity for the Baby Boomer Atlanteans and they were not ready to go through it as a complete group. Through Bush, the Atlanteans have set up a situation that is similar to what existed on Atlantis prior to their destruction. And now is the big choice—go left or go right—learn or don't learn. And they will do it as a group.

There will be some who will say they have not learned, and truly the success of the largest group Karma initiative on this planet is still unknown. But now the Atlanteans will elect a new leader and we will see if they opt for more of the same or if they opt for peace. Some would call Obama naive and say that his ideas are too simple and that he does not understand the complexities of world government. What he does understand is that there is much more to the planet Earth than just the United States, and his simplicity and optimistic approach will help heal many global wounds. As the new President, Obama will allow the Atlanteans to complete their period of group learning by proving they can have accomplishments without destruction, and he will allow the people of planet Earth to come together. This is important for the vibratory level of the planet to increase so that evolution can take place with less upheaval.

> *The reincarnated Atlanteans have been divided throughout this group incarnation. By finally learning their lesson and healing as a group, they will help bring a new period of peace to the Earth, without having to re-experience upheaval as devastating as the destruction of Atlantis all over again. The time is now to fix what happened to damage so many souls so long ago and that is the way it is with reincarnation."*

As the GG spoke about the large number of Atlanteans presently incarnated on the planet, I asked them if this was the "Baby Boomer" generation, and they replied that the majority of Baby Boomers are part of the Atlantean group, and some of them are Lemurian. I asked the GG what they meant when they said the Atlanteans have been divided throughout this group incarnation, and they replied that they are like two political groups where one has power for a time and then the other has power for a time. Then they said that in the 60's, one faction of reincarnated Atlanteans made a big push that didn't have immediate results but did shake up the country: The GG said that the" Summer of Love" and the entire "Flower Power" movement helped to change this country for the good—the "hippies" didn't bring about peace, but the ripple effects from 40 years ago are still being felt, especially in the areas of racial equality and equality between men and women. By openly questioning government leaders about war, people were challenged by new ideas. The "hippies," according to the GG, were a branch of the incarnated Atlanteans trying to make sure they learned their lesson and healed themselves in a peaceful way.

Regarding Al Gore, he wrote his book, "Earth in the Balance—Ecology and the Human Spirit" in 1992. Through this book and "An Inconvenient Truth," Gore clearly shows himself to be at the forefront of a movement towards global awakening. His concerns are not just for the United States, they are for the planet as a whole—and that makes it very easy for me to believe the GG when they say that as an Atlantean, Gore tried to put a stop to the destruction that was coming. And I hope the GG is right that Obama will be elected President and usher in a time of reparation and peace. By the time this book is published, the election will be over and we will know which direction the Atlantean Baby Boomers have chosen to take.

More about Reincarnation

"We reincarnate to learn, to grow, to make right things we have done in the past. So many throw the words 'Karmic debt' around as if they are a judge pronouncing a sentence on a guilty party. We ask you here to stop doing this. The truth of the matter is that we are our own judges and juries, and we personally decide what our 'punishment' will be—but to call it 'punishment' is not the right nomenclature. We don't punish ourselves, instead we create opportunities to learn from what we've done.

Regarding the 'debt' part, we help others now if we have wronged them in previous incarnations, and we help others because that is the right thing to do. No one is a tougher judge then we are on ourselves, and no one should go around pointing their fingers yelling 'Karma will get you!' Karma does not work like that. We review our lives, and we see where we went wrong. If we feel we have a debt to pay to another soul then we plan for that debt to be paid through service or an experience of some sort in a future incarnation.

We have spoken so much about so called 'bad' Karma that we feel the need to once again address 'good' Karma. Is there good Karma? Are we rewarded for being good? Treating our fellow travelers through time the way we expect and want to be treated is a very important part of our incarnations on this planet. Following the Golden Rule certainly helps us from creating additional Karma for ourselves! We have so much to do and so much to accomplish when we incarnate; we have cast ourselves in so many varied roles with such great expectations to complete all of the tasks that we set out for ourselves. All who are incarnated should worry about their own progress and not worry about another's Karma, as we are in no position to judge another's progress during their current incarnation.

It is the great hope of all who reincarnate to play their roles well, see their windows of opportunity early, meet their goals, and move to the next level."

Reincarnation: Some things to think about

- We each live multiple lifetimes—changing genders and races in order to learn and experience what we need for learning and growth of our soul.

- If we make mistakes or miss a window of opportunity, we will have similar opportunities during other lifetimes to acquire the learning we desire.

- As we work out Karma, we do it individually and sometimes with a group of souls with whom we have a reason to work together for the growth of the entire group.

- Karma is not how we punish ourselves, it is how we plan

opportunities for learning and growth within each incarnation.

- Following the "Golden Rule" will help us avoid additional Karmic debt.

- No one should attempt to judge another's progress.

CHAPTER FOUR
Relationship Villains

"We sit and plan our lives here on Earth. We are here with many entities, all of whom play many different roles in our many lifetimes, and our point today is that it is those who love us the most who will play the role of the villain. This is because they love us enough to want to make sure that we accomplish what we wish to accomplish for ourselves—even when it means being perceived as the bad guy!"

The information that the group shared about "relationship villains" was brand new to me, and I couldn't wait to hear more. In my opinion, when they introduced relationship villains, the Group took the study of Karma to a new level. As you read this section, please try to keep an open mind about the following possibilities:

1. We *have* lived before.
2. We *will* reincarnate.
3. Karma *is* instrumental in the planning and execution of each one of our lifetimes.

"The terrible things that go on, the 'villains' in your life, most times are really your most amazing friends because they are sacrificing so that you can learn and grow. Sometimes it seems as though we truly dislike or hate someone, but that entity in truth could be one of your most beloved friends outside of this incarnation—someone who loves you enough to do you a big favor."

I get chills every time I read this passage. Even though I absolutely know the truth of it in my heart, I still have a hard time with it in the context of my own life experiences. When someone's "done you wrong," you don't necessarily perceive them as having just done you a big universal favor! But this is the concept the GG is asking us to open our minds to and explore, starting with me. Recognizing someone who pushed me up against a wall and spit in my face as my "universal friend" is much easier said than done.

Relationship Villains & Romance

"As much as you dislike Jim, underneath you know that he was crucial in your awakening because you wouldn't wake up through lesser means. Bruce [my first husband] *and Joe (my second husband) and others all provided opportunities for you to awaken, yet you did not. Yes, you started to wake up, yes, you got so far each time, but you did not truly awaken until everything you believed in was being questioned and Jim tried to completely take over control of your life. You wouldn't allow it anymore and you started the next stage of your journey by taking control of your life and becoming truly independent instead of allowing others to rule your life. It was a huge step that took a lot of crap being hurled at you to get you to pop those eyes open. We maintain that you would have woken up in a kinder, gentler way had you stayed with Joe for just a little longer. You were on your way and didn't really have to experience the hard things you went through. But the bottom line is that you did it, and you woke up, you took back your power, and you moved on. The entity that is*

*currently Jim did that for you—he woke you up,
no, he shook you awake in a way where you could
not ignore it any more. You had to step up and
take action."*

To think that the one person in this lifetime that I dislike the most
could be one of my closest universal friends is still a hard pill for
me to swallow. And just ending that relationship wasn't
enough—Jim ended up working in my department's main office,
and I had to see him on a regular basis. Eventually he asked me
if I would sit down and talk to him, and he apologized for the
things he did. I accepted his apology, and I get that he did me a
favor, but let me tell you, it was hard to forgive. Now he doesn't
work at the same company, and I don't have to run into him
anymore—so maybe that final conversation of apology and
forgiveness ended our business together for this lifetime.

When Jeremy first announced to me that part of my "To Do"
list for this incarnation was to write a channeled book, I
remember thinking that there "had better be something new and
different to tell people." This concept of "Relationship Villains"
was certainly new and different for me, but it was very hard to
accept at first. Here's more from the GG:

Relationship Villains and Friendships

*"Let's move on to relationships that have troubles
or apparent troubles you see within them. It is not
strictly boyfriend/girlfriend or husband/wife
relationships that are Karmic. The bottom line
here is that souls come back with groups of other
souls with whom they have planned their lives and
planned the opportunities for growth that will
happen during those lifetimes."*

According to the group, relationship villains aren't just people with whom you have a romantic relationship, they can be friends and acquaintances as well. I had a very close friend, whom I loved like a sister, turn against me right after I left Joe. I confided in Jane that I was planning to end my marriage and the reasons why; and she decided that I was wrong to leave. While pretending to be my friend, she embarked on a covert "anti-Sherri" campaign that was hurtful personally and costly professionally. The more determined I was to get a divorce, the meaner Jane became.

As this was going on, Jane was promoted to a Department that I was also hoping to move up to. Twice in a 6-month period I was led to believe by the Directors of the department that the "next opening was mine." Without explanation, those promotions went to other people. It wasn't until about a year later, after Jane left the company, that I discovered why. She had sabotaged me both times! The first time, she set the stage by telling co-workers I was involved in Voodoo, and then convinced the Managers conducting the job interviews for the promotion that I was basically insane. She killed my opportunities for advancement by telling them things about me that were actually true, but she left out important information and twisted things to make me look crazy. One of the things she told management was that I said I was "from another planet." Actually, I did say that; it was at a dinner party at my house after a trip to Cassadaga (a town in Central Florida whose residents are spiritualists, mediums, and psychics). I was repeating something that a psychic had said to me about my soul originating in Arcturus. We were all discussing psychics and readings we'd had in the past, and she was very much a contributing participant in that conversation! I shared the Arcturus tidbit because I thought it was quite startling, and interesting because it's not the usual thing you hear during a reading. She certainly left out *her* part of that conversation, and twisted it perfectly to make me appear to be looney tunes.

Again, Jane and I were very close, like sisters, and she knew a lot about me. She based her voodoo comments on the fact that I work with herbs. At the time this all happened, I had just completed the requirements for an herbology certificate from the renowned herbologist, Rosemary Gladstar, and I was pursuing my N.D. (Doctor of Naturopathy) degree at the Clayton University of Natural Healing. So, with her clever twists on the truth, my homework assignments were turned into voodoo and witchcraft—not things that most employers want to see on a resume! And the revelations about the things she said got even worse—I was more than stunned by the implication that I sacrificed animals! I've been a vegetarian for more than two decades, I regularly contribute to several animal rescue charities, and I feed every cat, raccoon, squirrel, bird and opossum that steps foot in my yard! She was obviously very convincing, and when the managers who initially interviewed me for that promotion eventually told me why I lost those opportunities, they were extremely apologetic about it. And you know what? After learning what she said, I probably would have steered clear of me, too!

In the context of relationship villains, is Jane one of mine? Until all of this happened, I never felt like I had any "enemies," but afterward, I definitely considered her to be my enemy. Yet from a life-planning point of view, is Jane actually an entity so close to me on a universal level that she was willing to do seemingly terrible things to me during this incarnation? In retrospect, she did try pretty darn hard to get me to stay with my husband. And the GG have told me over and over again that I would have learned my big lesson much easier if I had stayed in that marriage for a while longer. Would she have turned on me eventually even if I had stayed married to Joe? It's hard to say from this side of the veil, but because of the things she did, I ended up with a promotion that was much better than the ones I previously lost. I became the first manager hired for a new department and I ended up progressing up the corporate ladder to

Director. Had I gotten either of the promotions that Jane sabotaged, I would have missed a fabulous job opportunity. The "relationship villain" concept makes me think of the term "frenemies" that I keep seeing in the paper about celebrities like Paris Hilton and Nicole Richie—friends in private, but enemies for the paparazzi. Even the GG have used this "frenemies" term in some of their dictation.

As I said earlier, the concept of relationship villains has been a difficult one for me. After meditating about it, I sat back and reviewed several pivotal moments in my life. In retrospect (and with that great 20/20 hindsight!), I think I can now name several "relationship villains" or universal "frenemies" who have helped me walk through windows of opportunity that I might otherwise have missed. It really puts a whole new face on things—this idea that people I thought "did me wrong" were actually helping me stay on my chosen path and cross stuff off my "To Do List."

Relationship Villains and Family

> *"The important thing to know is that an annoying or bothersome relative, or the one whom everyone might call the black sheep, is really the one who is the most giving because he or she has agreed to take on such a role so others can learn from the things he or she does. Do you follow?"*

I followed! The information dictated on this subject allowed me to look at my father in a whole new light. Always considered a "villain" by my sisters and I while we were growing up (and even still as adults), I now have new insight into precisely what kind of a "villain" he actually was and why. My guides have shared with me that my father was not part of the usual soul group that my sisters and I incarnate with—he popped over from *his* regular group to stir things up for us. He never did seem to fit in with the rest of us, and he spent a lot of time creating a volatile and unpleasant atmosphere for my family. If he was sent to "stir things up" for us, he did a great job. He abused drugs and alcohol, he constantly cheated on my mother, and he abused everyone in our family mentally and sometimes physically as well. As kids, my sisters and I never knew what to expect when we got home from school. Sometimes everything in our bedrooms was torn apart, the dresser drawers emptied, with everything piled in the middle of the floor—and he would be yelling at us to put it all away. What was he looking for? Who knows. At other times we would come home and there would be a bowl of penny candy or a bag of jelly donuts that he picked up for us on his way home from work that day. You just never knew if he was going to be the nice Dad or the crazy Dad. But from the outside looking in, he seemed like a really great guy, and he would bend over backwards to help people. I always thought he was one of a kind, and I was really surprised to learn from my friend, Debbie, that her father was just like mine. I was shocked when she opened up about some of her experiences with him, because from where I stood, he seemed like the greatest father in the world when I visited her at her house! Again, it's hard to forgive someone for doing the kinds of things that my Father did, but if you listen to the GG, I should thank him. Why? Because many windows of opportunity were opened by this entity, for me and for the rest of my immediate family.

Relationship Villains and Co-workers

> *"Let us turn to the current situation you are experiencing at work. There is a woman who is jumping on your idea and trying to take it over and be in charge of the project. The bottom line here is that by this action she is highlighting your idea and the others know who came up with the idea to begin with. Her brazen way of attacking the situation will not bode well for her. However, it will serve as a tool to further bring you to the attention of top management. Others were there*

*when you came up with the idea and it is being
pointed out to management that she has done this
kind of thing in the past. The question here is, is
she just another unpleasant co-worker or is she a
relationship villain who agreed to be the conduit
for things to happen due to her behavior? The
more important question is: How do you tell?' If
the work villain is to be spotted as someone in
your life who is really doing you a favor, then
consider the following things: Did she commit
her act of treason in front of others or behind
your back? If she did it in front of others and in
plain sight, she is most likely someone who
agreed to take an action to create a window of
opportunity for you and others to walk through.
Look for the window. If it was done behind your
back, it is an act for which there will be Karmic
debt incurred. Another way to tell is to look at
the history of the person. If they have a long
history of being in the frying pan, so to speak,
then they probably signed on for the role of villain
before incarnating. If they are someone who does
things like this once or infrequently, they
probably are just an unpleasant, conniving, co-
worker. Things will happen to right the wrongs
that are done—it's called Karma."*

The "current situation" discussed above is now several years old.
I remember being so mad at her for the way she was behaving in
a meeting, that for the first time in my career, I got up and walked
out of the room. I wasn't the only person she did this kind of
thing to, and I recall others standing up to her. I didn't stand up
to her, I just walked away—which means I probably missed that
window of opportunity, too. By the way, my idea-stealing,
trouble-making co-worker was eventually fired.

Relationship Villains & Bullies

I had a lot of experience with bullies in elementary school and in junior high school. I know the pain of being bullied, and I allowed bullies to make me behave in ways I wish I hadn't. There were times I caved in to peer pressure and there were times I resisted it, and if you were looking at a graph showing my popularity during my school years, you will clearly see where I resisted and where I gave in. I know now that I allowed Bruce, Jim and Joe to bully me, and I know now that I'm the one who allowed it to continue. I could have stopped it if I had recognized the windows, or asserted myself (without even realizing that the windows were there). The "bully window" was opened for me so many times that I'm sure this is an important item on my personal "To Do" list for this lifetime. Still, I was taken by surprise and not particularly thrilled when the GG added this subject to the table of contents for this book.

> *"Bullies are an ugly thing, but they are very much a planned occurrence for any given lifetime. When someone bullies you, you feel badly about yourself. Bullies stab at one's self esteem and make one feel they are not good enough or smart enough to fit in with the 'in crowd.' When a soul decides to be bullied in a particular incarnation it is usually because they want to work on building confidence and self-esteem. We can tell you, too, that the 'idea' of being bullied when you are at the planning table is very much different from the actual feeling of the experience during an incarnation. Many things that seem like they will be a breeze to go through when you're on the planning side of the veil, don't turn out to be easy once you are back in body.*

You will recall the time that your sister was being bullied and you made arrangements to meet the bully to put a stop to it. The bully never showed but you were willing to stand up to her for your sister. In that case it was a matter of one soul doing a little Karmic payback for another soul. Kathy had helped you in a similar matter in a previous incarnation. You did not want to fight! But you sucked it up and you showed up, and that helped to build your confidence—not as a fighter but as someone who will stick up for what's right even though it might get ugly. Do you follow?"

Wow! I remember that day very clearly. My sister was really being intimidated by this girl, and she had a reputation for fighting. I had never participated in a fight in my life. I think I was a Junior in high school at the time, and I turned to my friend Patty, who was very tough, for advice. She told me to spread the word that I was going to kick this girl's butt and get a buzz going. I followed her advice, had a huge posse of Juniors and Seniors accompany me to the chosen spot, and…the girl never showed up! And she never picked on my sister again either.

"Let us talk of your own experiences during your early school years. In elementary school, you were popular and then you befriended a girl that everyone made the target of intense ridicule. There was no good reason for this nonsense and you recognized this on a conscious level and on a soul level—you knew it was wrong to treat people like this. So what did you do? When your friends said, stop being friends with her or we will stop being friends with you, you chose your friends and you have felt badly about that ever since."

58

I remember this, too. "Dottie," as I'll call her for the purpose of this explanation, lived up the street and she was a nice girl. For some reason still unknown to me, kids said she smelled bad (she did not!) and called her by her name as if it was a dirty word. It was crazy. I spoke to her one day and I liked her. As soon as my friends saw me talking to her and found I had gone over to her house to play, that was it. They were very clear—it's her or us and believe me, they were quite prepared to turn my name into a dirty word too. I knew that dumping "Dottie" as a friend was wrong, and I knew my so-called friends were mean. But I didn't want to be unpopular. I didn't want to suffer what they put "Dottie" through. I never bullied "Dottie," but I didn't try to stop anyone, either. I'll tell you something wonderful here, though: In junior high school, "Dottie" just blossomed—she was one of the first girls to have a boyfriend and she had many friends. And the GG is right, I still feel terrible about not sticking up for her.

"And then what happened to you? In junior high you made friends with someone that everyone made fun of again. This time, remembering your elementary school experience, you didn't back down and you lost most of your friends. For two years you were very unpopular as they made fun of you just as they made fun of your friend. But this time you stood up for what you believed was right no matter what the consequences, which in your case was a nasty bout of unpopularity. In high school you were friends with many people from many different cliques and never again had to face the choice of one friend over another. Why? Because you walked through the window the second time it was open. It was difficult, it was painful, but you stuck to your guns and you didn't drop your friend. And having learned that lesson, you did not have to repeat it again in high

school. And what else happened to you from being bullied in junior high school? Did you not learn to value people for who they are and not the clique they were in? Has this lesson helped you in your life? You know that it has."

Well, that is the way it happened. But I have to tell the truth, and the truth is that those were two of the worst years of my life. That clique made my life miserable. I had my friend, that's true, but it was still torture. By the time high school started, the experience was basically over, and I had many friends in high school who were part of different cliques and groups, but the experience had a lasting impact on me. Even as an adult I would dwell on it and think of ways to get even with the people in that junior high clique. At one point I was going to write a book about a girl who murdered the people who made fun of her and then two things happened: (1) "Carrie" came out—so it was already done; and (2) at basically the same time, I got a message from my Guide, Jeremy, although I didn't realize it at the time, to basically "get over it." To me, it was like a thought bubble that appeared in my head saying to stop with the revenge plans already, dump the negative garbage, and move forward—that there was nothing to be gained and much to be lost by wallowing in self-pity. I was only unpopular for maybe two years, and I'm pretty tough, but a lot of damage can be done by a bully, as I learned first-hand.

One of the best jobs I've ever had was with the Periwinkle National Theatre for Young Audiences. Based in Monticello, New York, and in New York City, Periwinkle is an award-winning arts-in-education theatre company, and they travel around the world performing educational plays and doing workshops for elementary, middle, and senior high school students. My mentor, Sunna Rasch, founded Periwinkle, and while they have many important programs, my two favorites are "Halfway There," a drug and alcohol abuse prevention play that has won countless awards; and "Rooftop," a play authored by Scott Laughead. "Rooftop" helps kids understand how to deal with a bully, how to keep a bully from getting the best of them, how to assert themselves, who to turn to when being bullied, and it even touches on the feelings of revenge those who are bullied may harbor—all while helping kids learn that violence only breeds more violence and that communication is the key to solving problems. It's too bad I didn't see "Rooftop" when I was a kid! I don't think it was a coincidence that I came into contact with this play, and I found it comforting to know that the problem of bullies was getting attention and being addressed.

> "Being the bully is not a job that souls cherish and if you look at them, really look at them, you'll see that they have issues they need to overcome, and the role of bully gives them the opportunity to do so. The person who bullies you is most likely your 'universal frenemy,' because only someone who truly loves you would want to take on such a nasty role. Those that love us want to help us achieve our goals and our growth in the shortest amount of time possible. So Sherri, think about what happened when you were in your 20s. You were so hung up on those times in junior high school and wondering how you could plot revenge against those who had wronged you. What happened then? Fortunately, you were awake enough for Jeremy to come to you while you were sleeping and tell you that revenge was the wrong thing to do. And didn't you then astral travel and meet with the very souls who were part of the clique that bullied you? And didn't they apologize to you so you could put it behind you and concentrate on positive things instead of old windows that you went through successfully?"

Did I say at the start of this book that I needed to work on my fear of being considered a "weirdo?" I think the GG brought up the Astral Traveling to give me a nice big window of opportunity! Okay, I was definitely planning to leave this part out of the story, but here goes:

I was in a dark place when I was dwelling on that group of kids and what happened to me. I got the message from Jeremy (I didn't know that's what it was at the time), and then, in a "dream" one night shortly after, I found myself sitting down with the two ringleaders. They told me they were just having fun and didn't really mean anything by it. And then they apologized to me. I forgave them, by the way, and I moved on. It was a very vivid dream—it wasn't like a dream at all, it was as if I were actually there talking with them. The GG tell me that the three of us astral traveled for that meeting so I could move on with my life. I've had other experiences like that one where I've met with people or felt like I had really been at places I dreamed about. I remember one "dream" where I was in the Bahamas in a beautiful pool of the bluest water, surrounded by tropical fish! When the alarm went off, my whole body jumped! Here is some information from the GG about Astral Traveling:

"Let us talk this morning about astral traveling. It is not something to be undertaken without proper understanding. It is an excellent way to get around and see the world, but it is best if one understands the undertaking, as it is possible to be attacked by a lower astral plane being. Truly, there is no real danger but should it happen to you, you will find it to be a very scary phenomenon. There can be no death involved and no real harm, but if attacked you will have to fight or flee. The best thing to do is stand your ground or try to move upwards so you can take the lower

level entity to a higher level of the astral plane—it will not be able to follow you there.

Astral traveling is something that should not be undertaken lightly and it should be done to travel and see different places, or to help heal people, not to interfere with or scare other people.

For many, they astral travel during their dream state and don't know what they are doing.

As human beings continue to raise their vibrations, more will experience this in their sleep and consciously, too.

After this information was dictated, and I was told that I have a predilection for astral traveling in my sleep, I went to the bookstore and immediately bought a book on the subject: *The Llewellyn Practical Guide to Astral Projection* by Denning & Phillips. For those readers interested in pursuing this subject further, this book confirmed what the GG said, and gives the reader step-by-step instructions to how to "travel" consciously.

Relationship Villains & Politics

Note: this section was dictated two years before the section about the Baby Boomer Atlanteans.

"Relationship Villains can be people in high office or high positions who push their own agendas on others or seem to push their own agendas on others. Sometimes those villains are relationship villains carrying out missions that need to be carried out. Could there have been a crucifixion of Jesus Christ without Judas or Pontius Pilate? Was Pontius Pilate a villain or was he the tool by which the whole episode was allowed to take place? Would Bush have seemed a hero to so many if Bin Ladin hadn't executed

the attacks on the United States during Bush's watch? Is it possible, just possible, that Bush became president so that we could see that the time for war mongering is over and that a more peaceful operation of the United States and its foreign policy would yield better results?

At the time of 9/11, the majority of the people of the United States did not wish for war, but there was a prevailing wind at the time that if you didn't stand behind Bush and his call for war, you were un-American. Bush is a bully who likes to create animosity. But he is and has done a great job of calling attention to the negative effects of bullying, and the negative effects of violence as a means of achieving peace.

George Bush is a relationship villain for this time in U.S. history, and he is not alone. There are many relationship villains on a global level, meaning there are universal strings attached from person to person and country to country, and this is hard to see and understand while the veil is firmly in place. Once we see past the veil, or start to wake up, we will begin to see that there are connections everywhere, and we will become more aware of how these connections come together to form an intricate web of intrigue and everyday goings-on. There are no coincidences—this is fact. But there are connections—many, many connections—and as we wake up, we see them more and more and more."

Talk about there being no coincidences. I was startled by the GG's reference to Judas. In the Spring of 2006, I was organizing the dictated notes from the GG, and trying to put them in some kind of order that made sense, when I came upon their mention of Judas. I had pretty much made up my mind not to include it in the book—it seemed way too controversial to me. That changed on April 8, 2006, when my husband Ted and I were visiting our very dear friend, Heidi Winkler. Ted was helping Heidi put in her new sound system and I was reading the newspaper, waiting for them to finish so we could go to lunch. Much to my surprise, the *Orlando Sentinel* had a long article about a documentary that was going to be on the National Geographic station the next night, and guess what the subject was? It was about Judas, and the premise of the show was this: Was Judas doing Jesus' bidding when he betrayed him? I was floored by this article! It said that the lost "Book of Judas" had been found, and the information that was translated from it indicated that Judas was carrying out Jesus' orders. It was no coincidence that I saw the article about the Book of Judas just as I was considering leaving out the above section. I still think it's controversial, but I took the "universal hint" and left it in.

"Let us continue our discussion about relationship villains and the fact that this country is in a time of war; and what appears to be an extreme period of going back to the dark ages instead of going into the light. This is a time when much Karma is being purged and the end of darkness is coming. You know the saying, 'It is always darkest before the dawn?' Well, this is a short dark age that will be over very soon and then it will be a more peaceful world.

The people must take more of a global point of view, not just a polar 'this is my country and that's all that matters' point of view. It won't work anymore. We are all in this together and it's time to accept that and move on so we can take care of the Earth and fix the things we need to fix—as an entire population of humans, not as individual 'cells,' like we were terrorists protecting our own little pieces of land. Do you see what we are saying? The world is in a fix right now, but it's okay, it will be alright, we will come out of this.

That is the way with enlightenment and coming out of the dark. Each of us has our own dark age and then the world has a dark age. As more of us open to the light and open our eyes individually, so then does the world become a lighter and brighter place. More and more countries will begin to see the light in their part of the world. People will come alive, stop being automatons, and stop following so blindly in the footsteps of, or obeying the commands, of insane leaders. But then again, relationship villains—how can people learn to overcome and to wake up if they have nothing to prod them? That takes us back in the circle to the relationship villain actually being a good thing in many cases! We need them to prod us into action that we wouldn't take if left on our own!"

Relationship Villains: People who are Rude

"Let us talk about people who are simply rude and nasty all the time. They are negative and it makes a negative impact on those around them. This is a kind of relationship villain in that these people take on the personas you see in order to help those around them. It's all about how you react to this type of person, the ones who present challenges for those around them. They can be overbearing, rude, gossipy, pushy, all of the

things that you really don't look for in a friend! They are often our co-workers or people that we meet in the course of everyday chores and carrying out our business. The bottom line here is that they could either be adopting this type of persona for this incarnation because they have agreed to provide opportunities for others to step up and look the other way OR to confront them—depending on what is right for that individual's growth. Either way, there are windows and windows of opportunity surrounding 'rude' people. Another point we want to make regarding someone who seems rude or who is not following all the customer service rules we might expect of a service person or a co-worker is this: It could be that they have just suffered a loss or been through a trying experience. They may not have this persona all the time, but perhaps just at that moment in time, they have it for a specific reason. That gives those interacting with this person a window of opportunity. Even without knowing what's up with the person, you can either be polite and look the other way, or inquire why the rudeness and find out what's going on. Again, either way, it's a window and you can walk through it or you can shut it. If you tend to encounter a lot of rude people, as you sometimes do, it might be best to look at yourself. You might be attracting this to you because you haven't dealt with the situation properly in the past. This goes right back to what we said in the beginning of our dictation about how we continually attract situations to ourselves [life scripts] to help us learn a lesson. We here believe that if you would stop expecting people to be rude, if you would

> *start smiling as you are grocery shopping, that*
> *perhaps you will encounter more friendly people*
> *than rude people. Give it a try!"*

As you can see, the above passage contains a personal message for me to change my behavior—let me elaborate. I went through a period where people were banging into my shopping cart and just plain being rude to me every time I walked into the grocery store! It happened to me all the time and I remember thinking, "I'm a nice person, why are people so rude?" I tried switching grocery stores, but it still happened. Then one day, as I was lunching with my very good friend, Terri Marinaro, I asked her for her take on the situation—she has a way of getting to the bottom of these kinds of things. After Terri and I analyzed my behavior, and together we recalled some information given in Doreen Virtue's Angel books, I realized that these situations were not an accident—there was a window of opportunity and a lesson waiting for me at the grocery store!   I became aware of *my* personal behavior whenever I stopped to pick up a loaf of bread, and I suddenly realized that because I was always in a hurry, I tended to look down instead of looking people in the eye. I also noticed that I experienced something close to "cart-rage" when someone bumped into me or cut me off (obviously an extension of the road rage I also suffered from!). I then realized that I had begun to *expect* the people I encountered there to be rude to me!

I was definitely co-creating a rude reality for myself at the grocery store, so I tried an experiment. I told Terri that I was going to formulate a strategy (Doreen Virtue's Angel books have influenced me in many ways) where I would pretend that everyone in the store was an angel in human form waiting to test me, and I was going to treat *everyone* as if *they* were angels. I started smiling at people and nodding "hello" as I passed them. I gave others the right of way, even when they were cutting me off, and I smiled when I did it. I even started letting people with one or two items jump ahead of me at the check-out line, even though I was in a hurry myself. And it worked! The rudeness in the grocery store stopped for me, and it's very rare that anyone bumps me or cuts me off. When they do, I still pretend they are angels testing me and I smile at them, and I check myself to see if I'm the one who is being rude to other people without realizing it.

Relationship Villains—Summary

"Relationship villains: They are something people need to think about and to investigate in their own lives to figure out why they exist and how they can put an end to any villain situation. We can tell you, too, that when you confront a relationship villain, one of two things will happen: Either the relationship with that person will end because the project you two planned together is over OR you will continue a relationship that will be on a much more palatable level. There is no way to tell beforehand because it is something that is planned by each individual. A good rule of thumb is that if it is a family member, there will probably, but not in all cases, be a continuing relationship. If it is a friend, the relationship will probably end, but again, not in all cases.

It's all about the learning and the planning. There may be more left to learn from each other and so it will continue. That is why friendships end—entities come in to help each other with certain things that are short term and then they go away because there is no need to continue. It's not a nasty thing, or a mean thing, it's just a case of the time and purpose for that relationship has passed and it's the growing apart thing that humans talk about all the time. Now you know the reason for it."

I've often been saddened by the passing of a friendship and wondered why that happened. I've had friendships that simply ended when one of us moved or changed jobs, and a couple that ended with arguments that caused pain on one or both sides. One day you're the best of friends, and the next thing you know, you've gone your separate ways. Sometimes losing a friend is as bad as going through a divorce; sometimes you lose friends as well as a spouse when you divorce or separate from a significant other. I was glad to learn that this is a normal part of our lives, and it makes it easier, I think, to treasure past relationships for the joy they brought or the window(s) of opportunity they provided. And since this information was dictated, I've tried to keep my mind open to the possibility that when someone "does me wrong," so to speak, maybe he or she is really a close friend who has taken on a not-so-nice role to provide me with a window for learning and growth.

Relationship Villains: Some things to think about

- Often times, those we consider to be our enemies or whom we think "did us wrong" are actually our closest universal friends.

- Those who are closest to us will undertake difficult roles in our lives to help us achieve our goals during a given lifetime.

- Those who seem to be our enemies are often carrying out our specific requests in order to help us achieve our desired results.

- Windows of opportunity become much more "in your face" as you continue to miss them. This is to help us make sure we eventually wake up and seize one of the carefully planned opportunities for learning and growth we made sure to incorporate into our incarnation.

- Being bullied is a planned experience that is connected to a window of opportunity.

- Having the same type of experience over and over means that you are missing your windows of opportunity.

CHAPTER FIVE
Evolution

Prepare to be shocked yet again. I was riveted to my computer on the days that the Group chose to write about the subject of evolution. Did I say that I thought the Judas section was controversial? That reference is tame compared to this . . .

Evolution & Our Bodies

> *"The legend of where people came from, the Adam and Eve thing, is really not true at all. That is not how people inhabited the Earth. It is really a mix of two things. One is the soul or spirit that enters the body and the other is the body itself. Many bodies were tried for reincarnation purposes, and the body of the primate turned out to be the best bet for this purpose. Most people on Earth today inhabit bodies evolved from primates."*

Let me interrupt the GG here for just a moment. They started this session by saying that the story of Adam and Eve isn't true, and that's kind of a shocking statement. I don't believe in coincidences, but I do believe in synchronicity. It's July 2008 as I'm looking over this section before sending the final draft to Ozark Mountain Publishing, and I just read an article in the paper about a new PBS documentary called, "The Bible's Buried Secrets," which is due out in November 2008. By the time you read this, we'll all know what the hoopla is about, but according to the article I read, and the headlines it's already making, this documentary is going to be very controversial! From what I understand, it challenges the Bible's stories while at the same time explaining how and why the stories were told in the first place, how and why they were written down, and why they continue to be important to us. And this isn't the first documentary to address this subject—I saw a similar show on the History Channel a few months ago. The question of whether the Bible should be taken literally is suddenly very popular. The question is, "Why now?" Lee Carroll and Kryon explain synchronicity in great depth in the Kryon books, and my basic understanding of this concept is that synchronicity is a series of what appear to be coincidences, but they're not. They are planned occurrences timed to help us wake up and take notice. I think there must be something that we are meant to discover in or about the Bible at this time in our planet's history, and I think it's crucial to our evolution. It will be very interesting to watch what unfolds! Back to the GG:

> *"...As the primates evolved, so did the bodies that the spiritual entities inhabited. It is not a big deal this whole thing about what happened: Was there evolution or did God create Adam and Eve? The truth is simply that entities wanted to experience life on the planet and they could best do that in a body of this planet. The law of Karma came into being as more and more entities came to experience life on this planet, and interacted with each other positively or negatively. Reincarnation enables entities to work off past debts or to help others, and to learn and grow. The way the body arrived at its present state was through evolution, and here's the big news, it isn't going to stay this way either! No, no, no! It is continually changing and in fact, there will come a time when there will be no more male and female—it will be androgyny at its finest, and why not? Bodies will continue to change! Think about it! Many more 'gay and lesbian' entities are incarnating than ever before. These are the brave souls who are*

74

incarnating to help make the changes on this plant happen. Like the Indigo and Crystal children, they are so wide-awake and so tolerant of people being individuals, and being accepted for who they are. Sherri: gays, lesbians, Indigos, Crystals, Rainbows, these entities are of a higher vibration than most who are presently incarnated on the planet. These entities are on the front lines of the lightworker movement. And we say to you now that when people laugh at others for being 'overly sensitive' to the feelings of human beings, animals, and the planet as a whole, they are making a mistake. The entities who care about the underdog, who care about the so-called lesser life forms, and who care about the planet itself, are the entities who are on the front line."

Wow! You might recall that one of the reasons I pulled away from that Baptist church in upstate NY was because the pastor told us that the devil was "littering the earth with fake dinosaur bones" to make us believe in an evolution that never happened. I've always felt that the truth was somewhere in the middle of creation and evolution—that we just didn't know the whole (or real) story. I kind of like the idea that our bodies are still evolving; it makes sense that this would happen as we grow spiritually and as the vibrations on the planet reach higher levels.

Regarding the Indigo and Crystals the GG refers to above, as I mentioned in a previous section, I first learned about the Indigo, Crystal, and Rainbow children from Doreen Virtue's books and seminars. This is an area that I have not spent a lot of time studying, but as I understand it, the Indigos and Crystals are two new generations of children already incarnated on our planet. They are very sensitive, psychic, and more spiritually aware than previous generations. If you have children, are thinking about having them, work with them, or are even just around kids, you might want to read Doreen Virtue books—*The Care and Feeding of Indigo Children*, and *The Crystal Children*. They are well worth every moment you will spend reading them and will give you much greater insight than what is presented here by the GG.

The thought that super-sensitive people are not just "sissies" is something that I'm happy to include in this first book. It's also very easy for me to believe that folks who happen to be gay are on the front lines. It takes a true warrior for the light to plan a lifetime filled with sad, difficult challenges. I know that I would much rather hang out with people who care about other people, who care about animals and plant life, and who care about and want to help each other and our planet. Wouldn't you? I'll tell you a secret about me—after all, what do I really have left to hide, right? As time goes on, I think that I am becoming more and more emotional—the tears just seem to well up over just about anything sad or happy! I've mentioned it to some of my friends, and Diane Diaz, Grace Velez, Heidi Winkler, Shelly Koehler, Leigh Herr, and Irene Ayala have all told me that it's happening to them too. The fact that other people I know and trust are having the same experience led me to ask the GG about this tearful and somewhat embarrassing phenomenon. They explained to me that it's a side effect of the vibrational changes currently happening on our planet, and that many people are currently experiencing the same thing. I don't want to spend my days crying my eyes out, but if it's a bump up on the evolutionary path to a nicer and more peaceful planet, I'm happy to be overly emotional for awhile. Oh, come on, if you're reading this book, I bet you cry while watching commercials, too!

Evolution & The Cleansing of our Planet

> *"There will be changes to the surface of the world as well. There will be changes that will seem catastrophic to some, but to those in the know,*

*they will just be the continuous movement toward
the new age that has been heralded for so long.
The terrible things going on in the world are part
of a mass cleansing of the Earth. There is a lot of
Karma being used up right now. The debts are
being paid in a big way as the planet moves
toward a higher vibrational level where there will
be no cause and effect [Karma] to hinder the
occupants.*

*The world will become a kinder, gentler place.
Although it will take awhile to reach that stage in
terms of human years, it is really just the blink of
the universal eye.*

*So let us talk about peace. Peace on Earth
will happen, but the planet cannot evolve to a
place of peace until the entities living on her
evolve to a place of peace. For a great many
entities, there are things they need to do and feel
and experience in order to move on; but again, as
each new generation is born, there is less Karma
to overcome and we get closer to our goal.*

*Do you see where this is leading? What can
we do now to help achieve peace for the planet?
We can stretch ourselves further and further and
learn and wake up and become more educated,
because the more awake we become while
incarnated, the better off the planet will be and
the better off we will be when it's time for our
next incarnation! It's true! You will more quickly
get to the point you are at now in your next
incarnation, and that will happen each
succeeding lifetime until you have completed the
cycle of lives on the planet and you can move
on—all the while helping the planet to evolve as
well.*

The changes on Earth are normal and natural, and will continue. As the cleansing of Earth continues so shall the refinement of the human race. It is time to move on to the next level of evolution and there are those who are not ready for the changes taking place. The entire atmosphere will change and it will become charged with more and more positive ions as the shift in consciousness really goes into full gear. This evolution is happening as we speak and there is no stopping it. The war in Iraq and the terrorism around the world are the last vestiges of the old energy that will be summarily stamped out. You will see a new joy in the world and a new attitude. And it will all begin with the election of a new President of the United States. The feminine side of mankind is moving to the forefront now. The world will really see great strides over the next ten years and you will see your first woman president within the next ten years.

Think of it, a world full of positive energy and enlightened souls striving to help one another and the Earth.

You need to tell people that it is always darkest before the dawn, and that's the point we are at. It is the dawn of a new age and a peaceful age where the people of the world will start to come together as one. You are already seeing things happen with the whole outsourcing controversy, but this step is helping underdeveloped countries to grow and the United States will not suffer from the loss of these jobs. By helping underdeveloped countries, the consciousness of all will be raised as more people begin to live less difficult lives. The time for understanding of all peoples and cultures is at hand, and we have learned from this president [Bush] that you cannot bully other countries."

I think this is the first time the GG actually made a prediction—our first woman president within the next ten years! And it does seem to be the "darkest before the dawn" right now, doesn't it? We were so removed from terrorism until 9/11 and now it's part of our everyday lives—I barely ever thought of it, and now it's hard not to think about it every day. It's also hard to believe right now that a peaceful planet is in our future, but I think that outsourcing will help in that respect. I have never liked it when people put a greater value on the lives of the citizens of one country over another. It makes me very sad when people get mad at Angelina Jolie for adopting children from other countries when there are "children right here in America" to adopt. Is the life of an African or Cambodian child worth less than that of an American child? Is an American child more deserving of adoption than a child from China? I don't think so. If outsourcing contributes to the globalization of our economy, lessens suffering, and helps create a better way of life for people, I'm all for it.

Evolution & The Human Race

"Let us talk about the people who will be inhabiting the Earth after the shift in the Earth's energy occurs. World peace will eventually be achieved and there will be a global feeling to everything: all business, all decisions regarding this planet, and the UN will not just be window dressing anymore."
The time will come when all of mankind cares about each other and race will not matter. In

fact, people will revel in each other's differences and be happy for the opportunity to learn about different cultures without putting them down or feeling superior about them. And that is attributable to the souls who are incarnating now and will continue to incarnate over the next few generations.

Some souls had to wait to incarnate until the energy changes started because they could not survive in a hostile environment. Each shipment of souls to the planet has had a different aura or energy about them and it is constantly getting stronger. The Indigos, Crystals and the Rainbows who follow (and much more so the children of these soul groups), will be the strongest in the flow we have experienced here on this planet. They will take the lead and make the changes and face the problems head on and we will feel and see the new energy emerging."

I don't have any children, but many of my friends do, and they tell me that their children seem very intelligent for their ages, and they ask questions that seem to be beyond their years. What parent doesn't think their child is special, right? But seriously, I've interacted with my friends' kids and they do seem very much like miniature adults to me. They want to know why they're being asked to do something before they do it—it's not that they're argumentative, they just want to understand the situation. Again, I don't have kids, nor do I have any training in child development, but it seems to me that this is a trait that you might see in pre-teens, not in three, four, and five year olds. Unless they are Indigos and Crystals. I think it's refreshing and it gives me great hope for the future whenever I'm around these kids. My feeling is that if they won't do something without understanding the "why" of it when they are so little, they will be very discerning when it comes to choosing the future leaders of our world. And that truly gives me great hope for the future!

> *"A new Earth is emerging and no longer will we have to endure the pain and trauma of incarnations that we experience now. But again, we say to you that each incarnation is a learning experience and chosen by the entity experiencing it because it is a way to atone for a Karmic debt or a way to advance by learning and feeling. Only by feeling and experiencing can entities be in a position to help others with like challenges. That is why some entities with no reason whatsoever to experience abuse, will choose to experience it. So that in the next lifetime, or in-between lives, they can counsel and help others to overcome their bouts with abuse. It's all education—that's the bottom line on this planet. But the planet and we will evolve and it will become a planet of peace, and incarnations will be a time of great learning without the pain and suffering."*

I like to think that I'm pretty strong and can handle whatever life dishes out by reminding myself that I planned it all, and there's something to be learned from the daily obstacles and situations I encounter. But there is one thing that I have a terrible time handling, and that is the death of a loved one or a pet. I just go to pieces, even though I know it's part of life, part of the plan, and that I'll see them at the planning table for the next go around. I asked the GG about this, and they indicated that we will eventually evolve to a place where souls will simply depart when they have finished their experience, without long illnesses or disease, and that leaving an incarnation will be a time of celebration rather than mourning.

"The time line for the change in the Earth's energy is not an exact science. There are lightworkers already in place on the planet and there are those being born who will carry on the work the first brigades of lightworkers started. The lightworkers are like an advance brigade of soldiers in the movement to bring peace to the planet. They have the hardest jobs because they are in a truly hostile environment, and often draw fire to themselves.

With more and more adults and lightworkers having Indigo and Crystal children, and as the Indigos and Crystals have their own children, that is when the planet will really see the change in the energy—for the energy that is being changed has to come from the human race. They must change individually and collectively in order for the planet to cleanse itself of all the negative vibrations that lace its atmosphere at this time."

After receiving this information, I asked the Group if they thought that one person really could make a difference and their answer was, "Absolutely!" I remember seeing a bumper sticker once that said something about "random acts of kindness," and I think it applies here. When someone needs to talk, and you listen to what they have to say, you've made a positive gesture that helps raise the planet's vibrational level. When you stop to help someone change a tire, you've made a positive gesture that helps raise the planet's vibrational level. When you rub your spouse's tired feet at the end of the day, you've made a positive gesture that helps raise the planet's vibrational level. You can come up with your own examples here, the possibilities are endless, but the bottom line is this—do nice things, help people out, and you are contributing to making the planet a better place. We can do this one person at a time; each helping to make a difference in the lives of those around her, and for the future of the planet.

> *"Again, we caution that there will be those who cannot stand the new energy; many now are starting to feel out of place as the energy begins to change, and some are reacting in truly violent ways and they don't know why or what's going on with their lives. They are just very unhappy. They cannot take the new energy and they are lashing out. Those individuals will adjust or move on. It seems sad but it has to happen in order for the Earth to evolve and for humanity to evolve to the next step. Those souls who check out early will have the opportunity to be reborn once their vibrational level is again compatible with the planet."*

After receiving this passage, I asked about tragedies like Colombine. The GG said that tragedies involving multiple souls departing at the same time are nearly always planned by those entities to create windows of opportunity for others, and the person pulling the trigger is nearly always a relationship villain doing the dirty work to carry the plan of action to fruition. There is always room for freewill, so some tragedies are unplanned, thus creating Karmic events. The Guides went on to say that many of those who choose to "check out" early are reacting to changes in the vibrational levels of the planet, and many do so by attracting terminal illnesses, such as cancer, so they can depart earlier than originally planned. Some don't go that far, and instead become withdrawn and depressed, and others engage in abusive or violent behavior.

> *"There are lightworkers covering the globe, and they are acting as beacons for the light to come to*

the Earth to be absorbed into the Earth, making it more and more difficult for people to allow things like terrorism to continue. You see, a large number of people simply will not stand for it any longer. At some point over the next generation or two, there will be enough people on the planet who will not allow or tolerate such activities, and they will overpower those who would do it. The atmosphere and vibrational level of the planet will have changed and evolved to the point where violence will not be tolerated."

This is what I meant earlier when I said that the Indigo and Crystal children give me such hope. They and their children will have more of a backbone when it comes to standing up for the right thing, and what's best for the planet. My husband, Ted, turns on the news as soon as he gets up every morning, and he watches the news every night from 6:00 – 7:00 p.m. I always leave the room. It's not that I don't want to know what's going on in the world, I do, but to see and listen to the same negative sound bites over and over and over again, is just too much for me—which is why I read the paper to get my news. I can't stand to see the violence on TV—it's different than reading about it. This is pure opinion on my part, but I believe that violent video games and violent footage on TV and in the movies has made many kids and adults immune to what pain and suffering really is.

I'm glad to know that this planet will eventually institute a zero tolerance policy regarding violence, and I think a great way to work towards that end would be to immediately stop buying violent video games for ourselves and our kids.

Evolution & Connecting to the Source

"We go today to the subject of what will become of the human race. Where is it all going? The fact of the matter is that the human race is evolving, ever evolving, to a place where enlightenment is an everyday state of being. That is what we are reaching for—to be one with the creator on a consistent basis. Not to reach it during a single yoga pose or during meditation for a brief moment or two. That is not what we are looking to achieve!

We want to connect and stay connected because that is where the source of all of our light and our life force stems from—from the Source, the Creator, the thing called God, which is neither male nor female, nor in any form that we know. Adam (and we) were not shaped after God! We were shaped as the primates we utilized in the beginning and evolved into our current bodies!

So, how do we get there—how do we become ever-connected to the Source? We already are! Part of the new evolution is recognizing we are now and always have been connected to the Source. We must recognize that the Source is simply that—the Source of all things: the Source of all beings, the Source of all planets, and the Source of all galaxies. Every atom that exists was made by the great Creator, the Source of all that is. Once we recognize this and acknowledge the truth of it, we can move forward and begin to achieve a oneness that will bring us much joy while we are incarnated on an otherwise fear-filled planet.

To achieve oneness with the Source, one needs only to close ones' eyes and look inside. Go inside because the Source is part of us all and we are part of the Source. We are all sparks of the Source sent flying out into the universe to spread our wings, learn, grow, and re-connect.

Now do not misunderstand us, we are NEVER DIS–connected from the Source! But we are, many of us, asleep when it comes to recognizing the Source within.

We must awaken ourselves and recognize that every one of us incarnated on the planet is a part of the Source. That is why we are called the brotherhood of mankind! We are all part of the same family, from the same creator—The Source!

We left off talking about what is up for the human race and what needs to happen to evolve into more spiritual light-type beings. Again, it is not hard, just long in the length of time it will take to accomplish it. But there are entities now incarnated, and those who will incarnate in the future, who are and will continue setting the stage for the transformations to come.

Each generation stretches a little farther and eventually the transformation will be complete. Think about it—how far has the human race come from the medieval ages? I know you don't think it has come very far, Sherri Ann, but it has come very far, and it goes further each generation. There are more vegetarians now than ever before! There are more people thinking about world peace now than ever before!"

I hope the GG is right and that more people are thinking about the moral implications of their actions. I was glad to hear that more people are thinking about world peace now than ever before, but being the "driver" personality that I am, I don't believe that "thinking" about it is enough. But how do we bring it about? What can we personally do to bring a little more peace to the Earth? I've given this a lot of thought, and I think we should start with ourselves. We can be nicer to each other at home and at work; we can watch our tempers (yes, I know this is the pot calling the kettle black!). We can follow the Golden Rule and treat everyone the way we want to be treated. I believe that cutting down on the amount of negative vibrations we put into the atmosphere will help us stop assaulting each other and our precious planet. And it will give the positive vibrations being pumped into the atmosphere a chance to develop and expand. Taking steps that help unite the world instead of dividing it will go a long way, too. I really believe that the current trend toward adopting children from different nations is eventually going to help this country become more global in its views. Those kids aren't going to stay kids forever, and my gut tells me that many of them are Indigos and Crystals. I know when my friends Shelly and Joe Koehler adopted their little girl, Emma, from China, they had to spend a lot of time learning about the Chinese culture before they were allowed to bring their daughter home. I know their son, Ethan, is learning about his sister's culture, too—how can he not? It seems clear that the more we know about other cultures and the more connections we have to them, the less likely we are to go to war. Could this trend of inter-continental adoption be part of a universal plan to help bring peace to the planet? Time will tell.

Evolution and 2012

All the talk of planetary changes and the vibrational level of the planet changing made me think about "2012." There have been many TV shows about it lately, and lots of chat on the internet. 2012 is the end of a 26,000 year cycle when the Mayan calendar ends, and according to Dan Eden's article for ViewZone, titled, "The Real Doomsday," on December 21, 2012: "The ecliptic of our solar system will intersect with the Galactic plane, called the 'Galactic Equator' of the Milky Way." I've read a lot of articles and watched many television shows about 2012, and what this means, as far as I can tell, is that the planet is going to shift in its orbit. And that, no matter how awake you might be, is a very scary thought.

I looked up "2012" in Wikipedia, and here's what I found: "2012 is sometimes claimed to be a great year of spiritual transformation (or apocalypse). Many esoteric sources interpret the completion of the thirteenth B'ak'tun cycle in the Long count of the Maya calendar (which occurs on December 21 by the most widely held correlation) to mean there will be a major change in world order."

So what do we do? Keep saving for retirement or go out and blow our paychecks every week? Before blowing my savings account, I asked the GG for some insight into 2012 . . .

"And now let us talk about 2012, that very important date that is being bandied around now and scaring the pants off of so many people. 2012 is an historic date, there is no doubt, but you will not see the planet destroyed or turned into a chunk of ice. It is the end of one age or cycle and the beginning of a new age. The changes leading up to the culmination on December 21, 2012, have been going on for a very long time. It is what lightworkers are working on, it is what beings from other planets are working on, and it is what so many on this side of the veil are working on. The first major movement to help prepare the planet for 2012, was started in the 1960s with the so-called 'flower children.' The flower children were Baby Boomers, and Baby

Boomers are primarily reincarnated Atlantean souls here to work out group Karma and attain healing for their part in the destruction of their own continent and the effect that destruction had on the entire planet. They wanted to be here now to assist in the planetary changes taking place.

This group rebelled against their parents and the establishment and although they failed to prevail in their 'make love not war' campaign, they still made very important inroads and helped to raise consciousness about our treatment of each other and the planet Earth. The Baby Boomer Atlanteans are at an age now where they are in positions of authority and they are the establishment! But they were the ones who fought the first big fight, the hardest fight because they were really looked down upon by their parents, their peers and the government. Being a flower child or hippie was a brave thing to do, to fight and protest against an unjust war—and they were there on the front lines. Their brave work paved the way for the next generation of lightworkers being born to make further progress, and they made it possible for the vibration of the planet to be raised to the extent that Indigo and Crystal children could be born here. The Indigos were the next big push to raise the vibrational level of the planet and help change humankind to prepare for 2012. Their children, the Crystals, are making even bigger changes to our vibrational levels, and the children of the Crystals are born awake.

The year 2012 will bring changes, but again, preparation for these changes were started many years ago. The changes happen gradually but the bottom line here and the thing to know and understand is that it is a date that promotes freedom. It is freedom from being in the dark, it is the freedom to live wholly in the light. Do not be afraid of 2012. Embrace it for what it is and do not allow yourself to go to the dark side thinking negative thoughts of fear and hoarding supplies and that kind of thing. Changes will happen, they are expected to happen and the best thing that incarnated humans can do is to continue to grow and learn and help to bring more light to the planet Earth. The more light that is brought to the planet, the higher the vibrational level of the planet, the easier the shift will be. And with this shift comes accelerated evolution for humans who incarnate on planet Earth. We are evolving to a level where humans will be born awake with knowledge of who they really are—do you see how this will lessen the struggle to learn and grow while incarnated upon this planet?"

And with that question the GG ended their dictation for the day. I love the thought of "being born awake," and I understand that all of us who are here now signed on to be here during this time of great change. Part of me feels that it's probably a privilege to be chosen to be here at this time. But it's still scary to me. The GG continued with more about 2012 the following day.

"There will be planetary changes, but these changes are natural and have occurred before on the planet as it evolved. It is difficult to say exactly what changes will occur because we don't know what the vibrational level of the planet will be in 2012. What we do know is that the higher the vibrational level, the less planetary changes or geographical changes will take place. Do you

understand? This is why it is so important for the lightworkers to continue to bring light to the planet. This is why the Indigos and Crystals, those assisting from other planets, those working on the project from this side all must continue to do their job—it's a big mission. And it is why all who are incarnated on the planet should try their best to be positive and optimistic and nice to each other, because even if they don't believe in all this new age mumbo jumbo, they will still help bring light to the planet.

The term 'new age' is just that—a term. It is not necessary the best term and maybe it has been used too often and ridiculed too often, but for the purpose of this discussion, we will use the term 'new age.' There will be a new age, and that said, we must all take our part in it very seriously at this juncture in history. Lightworkers on the planet will make much progress if they lead by example. When people see you living your beliefs instead of simply preaching to them about your beliefs, they will pay more attention. That attention alone will help increase the vibrational level.

And since lightworkers are merely bringing light to the planet, there is no religious philosophy or mantra for them to preach to anyone. Lightworkers try to do what is right—look around you and you will see them—they are the ones in the forefront of the changes, they are the ones driving hybrid cars, recycling garbage, looking for alternative energy sources, and picking up garbage on the side of the road. You will never see a lightworker tossing garbage or cigarette butts out of a car window!

Today's lightworkers are often ridiculed for their efforts to get people to 'go green,' just as the lightworkers in earlier decades were ridiculed when they marched for peace and equality. But this is the way with a lightworker, and this is the way that change occurs. Someone has to make it happen, someone has to be on the front lines and it takes a very brave soul to be on the front lines. Do you want to know what a Lightworker looks like? Look around you—look for women who are pushing through the glass ceiling—look at Hillary Clinton, Madelyn Albright, and Condoleeza Rice—all putting themselves out there on the front line and making it possible for women to continue to climb the political ladder. But would they be where they are today without the efforts of Geraldine Ford and others? Look at Barack Obama running for President—would this have been possible without the earlier efforts of Martin Luther King, Jr. and the brave souls who marched for civil rights? Could these people be in their positions of power today if it weren't for those that came before them, stood on the frontline for change and pushed the envelope? Lightworkers! They push the envelope! Lightworkers are on the front lines helping to make the 2012 transition as painless as possible for the planet and people who live on it."

As this section was completed, I thought, "What can I possibly add to this section that would give it more impact than it already has?" We were pretty much given our assignment. But as it turned out, there was more to come for this section! In October 2008, the Guide Group had more and updated information about the shift, and fortunately, the Publisher of this book was able to add it in before we went to print.

> *"Let us continue with the ballyhoo about 2012. We have written about it before and we believe this is a subject that needs to be addressed further and in more depth. First of all the date 2012 is not written in stone. When the planet is ready, it will shift to the fifth dimension. The Mayan's stopped their calendar at 2012 because it was the end of a cycle and because at that time, 2012 appeared to be the date for the shift. But that was a very long time ago and many things have happened since then that have influenced the timing of the shift, and are happening today that will influence it, and things that can happen tomorrow that will influence it.*
>
> *There will no doubt be a shift in the dimension of the planet at this time, and the planet itself and many of those souls incarnated on her will shift to the fifth dimension. What is unknown is exactly when it will happen and what the difficulties will be for those who must endure this shift. Some will shift with the planet and others will remain behind to continue their work. There will be great joy, but also great shock and sadness for those who make the shift to the fifth dimension, as families and friends look for each other and find that they are separated. For those who do make the shift, they will find themselves in a different type of body as the human race undergoes this next step in its evolution."*

The GG didn't dictate anything further about the new body, except to refer to it several times as a "light body," and to note that the human race would have this type of body after the shift to the fifth dimension. In Dolores Cannon's 3-volume series, *The Convoluted Universe*, there are many mentions of the human race having a light body when the planet makes the shift. This is particularly covered in "The New Earth" chapter of *The Convoluted Universe - Book Two*, where I learned that our light bodies will be longer and lighter than what we have now, and we will actually seem younger!

The GG continued their additions to the 2012 section with the following:

> *"Human beings are already starting to look at each other and make judgments about who will or will not shift to the new dimension. What will happen is that many they didn't expect to make the shift are there with them in their new light bodies, and some they thought would transition will still be in the 3rd dimension. Sherri, you must tell people that it is no one's business but the individual soul entity whether they transition with the shift or not. The bottom line is that not everyone is supposed to transition at this time. Some will not be ready. Their energy levels will not allow it and they will have more to learn before they can enter the next dimension. And that is okay! There is nothing wrong with this! This is not something to be judged and talked about. Each soul presently incarnated on the planet Earth should worry about him or herself, and make sure they are doing everything in their individual power to bring and hold the light on this planet. For in doing so, they will assist the shift and make it easier for those who are left behind. Are we making ourselves clear? This is an important message that we want you to get out to the Lightworkers: Do not judge others.*

There are many lightworkers incarnated now that could be doing more. They have dimmed and this is not the time to have a dim lightworker! We must all step up now and open our eyes and become awake to our individual missions so that we can ease the planet into its birth in the fifth dimension. The more the lightworkers come together and shine and do their jobs, the better off and the easier the transition will be."

Knowing that many of us are still wondering exactly what our particular mission is, I asked the GG how to determine our mission and what we can and should be doing at this time.

"So you ask us, as you should, what are the lightworkers supposed to be doing? How do they know what they are supposed to be doing? That is such a difficult question to answer as everyone is different, with a different mission and path. Meditation and paying attention to the little voice inside are two ways for lightworkers to find and stay on their individual paths. But the one thing they all have in common is to hold the light, to attract the light to the planet and hold it here, for the more light—the easier the transition. And how do we attract and hold the light? By being of the light, by acting as if we are of the light, and that means making changes to the way we do things. Stopping the road rage, stopping the rudeness and stopping the violence are three very good ways to get started. If each individual takes responsibility for spewing less negativity out into the world, more light will make it to the planet. Sherri, do you see that each person incarnated now can do so much by doing so very little?

Again, we say to you that people must watch what they say and do at this very important time. The more positive energy that is put out there, the better off all will be, and it is very important for people to start to monitor their thoughts. Thoughts are extremely powerful things. There is nothing that exists that wasn't first a thought. Things manifest slower on the planet Earth than in other places, but they still manifest. You have seen this yourself with things you've wished for that suddenly appeared. Those were pleasant surprises, my dear, but the reverberation of negative thoughts and vibrations is not so pleasant. As many will see, thoughts are becoming things at a much faster rate and so we must all watch what we say and think. We cannot emphasize this to you enough."

I understood exactly what the GG was talking about with their reference to my wishing for things that appeared. I've noticed in the last year that things I've seen in magazines that I liked but didn't want to spend the money on have miraculously appeared on my doorstep. I'm not talking about houses or cars here, but I've received several books and small items that I remember seeing on TV or in a catalog or magazine and thinking, "Oh, I want one of those!" And then I forgot all about it. And days or months later, someone would give me or buy me these things without me having said a word about it. It's happened to me enough times now that I am really starting to believe that we can manifest things that we want. And with that happy realization, comes the scary realization that the negative thoughts can come into being just as quickly and easily as the positive thoughts. The GG continued with more about the shift:

"To be a lightworker is a difficult thing. Lightworkers know they are different and they know they have something to do. While they wait to figure out exactly what their particular part of the mission is, there are things that everyone can do to make the shift easier.

1) *Be positive in your thoughts, words, and actions.*
2) *Don't judge other people—no one on your side of the veil can possibly know what is really going on with anyone else's incarnation. They should try to figure out what's going on with themselves instead.*
3) *Stop gossiping—it's not good for anyone.*
4) *Stop being rude—it spews negativity into the atmosphere.*
5) *Stop plotting against others—these dramas do no one any good and add to the negativity in the atmosphere.*
6) *Stop looking for underlying insults in what other people say to you, and stop insulting other people. All are on their individual path. You don't know what it is. Just because they don't meet your current standards does not make them wrong.*
7) *Start looking for ways to be nice to people, including, but not limited to, saying "good morning" or "good afternoon" or "good evening," when you see people.*
• *Smile at people. A nice smile or even a half smile will help as you pass people during the day. Smiling perks people up. The one who is doing the smiling and the one who is smiled at will both incur positive energy from the act.*

- *Say nice things if you can say them in a sincere way. Don't make things up, but look for things that you admire about others and give them a compliment. It brings positive energy to the person saying it and the person receiving it.*
- *Hold the door open for someone when they need it.*
- *Give someone else the parking spot when two of you are trying to get it at the same time. It is the little things like this that you can do every day without taking any time that will help you hold the light while you bring more light down.*
- 8) *Stop sweating the small stuff. If someone cuts you off in traffic or beeps their horn at you, don't give in to the negativity of the moment. Look at those moments as challenges and opportunities to hold the light. When we return negativity in moments like those, we spill some of our light.*

And here is what will happen when you put these simple things into practice and they become habit. You will change. You will become a nicer person. People will want to be around you more because they will sense the light within you, and most importantly, you will be helping increase the vibrational level of yourself, others, and the planet, which in turn will help the planet make the shift in an easier manner. One smile will have far-reaching effects!"

There is a phrase called "The Butterfly Effect" that was initially coined with regard to weather; i.e., a butterfly flapping its wings in South America can affect the weather in Central Park. This came to mind the other night as I was watching the television show, "Heroes," and one of the characters was explaining to another how going back in time is dangerous because it could change things drastically. And she said, "Step on a butterfly today and millions die 20 years from now." That's an indication of how one negative action can lead to a bigger negative reaction. But on the flip side, is it possible that doing something as simple as smiling can help raise the vibrational level of the planet? Within days of receiving this information, I decided to put it to the test and I started smiling at people in stores, in parking lots, and in the hallways at work. I even started smiling at my husband more! I can tell you this much—there wasn't one person that I've smiled at who hasn't smiled back. Some seemed surprised to be smiled at, but then their faces lit up a little bit. And I felt better each time I smiled. I may have internally smirked a little bit when the GG first wrote about smiling, but I now believe that a smile is very positive and powerful.

> *"Knowing that the shift will occur no matter what, it is a done deal, we must do what we can to make it easier for all concerned. Some will shift with the planet when it goes to the fifth dimension, others will stay behind. This is nothing to worry about or be upset about for all is as it should be. Some are ready to go and some are not ready to go. All will make the decision for themselves Some will feel badly for those left behind, but they are not really being left behind. They are simply on another level of growth and development, and the time is not right for them to shift. They would not be comfortable on the new vibrational level, and that is okay.*
>
> *Everyone on this planet now, whether they are shifting or not—and those decisions are being*

made by each of us individually, can assist in the shift and make it easier for all.

Let us all be positive in the face of adversity. When things happen that are not happy things or things that cause us grief, let us examine them and understand that they are part of the overall plan of many individuals. We need not understand another's life plan or even our own to know that there is something greater than ourselves at work.

Looking for little ways to bring more light to the planet will be baby steps that will bring big results."

Since the GG was continually bringing up the subject of the shift, I decided to ask about something that had been weighing heavily on my mind. What about the animals? I love animals. Throughout my life, I've had dogs, rabbits, and now cats as pets. I have cardinals, woodpeckers, blue jays, and lots of other birds visit my house every day, along with squirrels, opossums, and raccoons. The thought of precious animals suffering during the shift is something that continually brings tears to my eyes.

"You are concerned about the fate of animals during the shift to the fifth dimension. We can tell you that there will be animals making the shift along with humans. Some species will evolve and some will remain. Those species that do not evolve will continue on with their lives here or on another planet. Some will become extinct. It is not always a bad thing when a species becomes extinct. It certainly would be a different world today had the dinosaurs survived! When animals are threatened because of the conduct of human beings, that is a karmic debt that has to be paid. But sometimes evolution dictates that animals

100

change, just as human beings have changed during their evolution. Certainly modern man is a far cry from his early ancestors. Do you follow us? When the shift occurs, there will be humans who evolve and there will be non-human species who evolve and change. Do not fear for those who do not survive the shift—it will be but a moment in time and they will be back on the other side of the veil resting and deciding what they will do in their next incarnation. There is nothing to be done about this for any species, including human beings. Some will go and some will stay, and some will find themselves on the other side of the veil. It is simply the way it will be. But again, we take this opportunity to say to you and everyone reading this book, that now is the time to pay great attention to what you are thinking, doing and saying. For these things will be what helps to ease the shift for all."

I could not bring myself to ask the GG if they knew which species would evolve and which would not. This is one of those things I just don't want to know because if they told me that my cats aren't making the shift, I would have a very hard time being positive every day. Since receiving this information, I continue to smile at strangers and give up great parking spots. It's the least I can do! The GG ended their dictation about the shift with the following admonition:

"Dear girl, thoughts will become things much more quickly than in the past and we are at a time when our words and our actions have meaning that is 10 fold what they have ever meant before. This is a time of great acceleration and we can accelerate the light and bring it here much

quicker, thanks to all of the entities who are here now to attract and hold the light in the name of the planet Earth and for the ease of the shift. This is an exciting time! It is also a scary time for many and as you so want to say to people, 'knowing doesn't make it any easier.' But you cannot go around all day worrying about your cats and the birds and the dogs and the raccoons, and every living creature on the planet. If you want to make a difference for all inhabitants of the planet Earth, Sherri, then mind your Ps and Qs and pay attention to what you think, say, and do, for doing so will help all have an easier transition."

Evolution & Vegetarianism

That this subject came up at all was surprising to me. I've been a vegetarian for more than 20 years, and no one was LESS supportive of my decision to "go veggie" than my Grandmother. The very same Grandmother who now, as part of my GG, is pro-vegetarian! It hasn't been easy being the only vegetarian in a family of carnivores, and I make it a point to respect other people's choices—freewill is freewill. But it's not easy for me to watch other people eating animals. My conversion to vegetarianism came as I was thumbing through a magazine and came upon an advertisement about veal and how veal calves are treated. I remember going into the bathroom and crying my eyes out for an hour, and I still cry to this day when I think about how animals are mistreated. From that day on I never ate meat of any kind again. Initially, I thought it would be okay to eat seafood since I was still under the illusion at the time that fish were free-range. About a month after my decision to give up meat, I recall being out to dinner at a restaurant in St. Marten, sitting at a table overlooking the water. As the waiter delivered the mahi mahi to the table, I glanced out the window and saw a school of beautiful little fish swimming and playing. And then I realized that I was about to eat one of those beautiful creatures. I pushed that plate away and since that moment I've never eaten anything with a face or a mother.

"Sherri, let us tell you more about the future of the planet when all species will cohabitate—the way it once was, and the way it will be again. First of all, we know you have a problem with eating meat, and frankly, we do too. It interferes with the development of the spirit. It is violent and it brings fear into the body, and it's just plain not nice, is it?

Well, the animals who incarnate know what will happen to them and they've agreed to be part of the food chain in this way. But the high road is definitely to not eat meat. Those who abstain are practicing non-violence, and this is something far better for the soul and also for the health of the body. No one ever suffered Karma from eating meat, because again, animals understand what is going on when they enter, but those who treat animals unkindly will incur Karma. Vegetarianism is part of the movement towards a peaceful planet.

Within six to seven generations, we will once again stop being carnivores and the entities that are incarnating now onto the planet will help to make this happen, and at the same time peace will prevail on the planet. When you eat meat you ingest the fear those animals felt at the moment of their death. Fear makes people paranoid and fear is ingested by the person who eats the meat. As less people eat meat, there will be less skirmishes and less war. It sounds like PETA propaganda but it is not!

Sooner or later all will be vegetarian on the planet, but for now, don't despair because the animals are aware of what is going on and while we wince at the thought of hurting an animal and eating it, it is the current way of the world. But the world IS changing. Open your eyes and you will see this evolution is taking place as more and more people become aware and awake and watch what they eat and become vegetarian because of their love for fellow non-human entities on this planet. That is the way of evolution and it is part of the plan, so don't be mean to carnivores, just be a shining example and live according to your principles."

Back in the late 80s, there was a TV show called "China Beach" about nurses serving in Vietnam during the war. I will never forget the episode where a new nurse, upon arriving at her base, decides to go shopping in the village. She stops at a booth where there are lots of adorable puppies in cages. She decides to adopt one and points to the one she fell in love with. The proprietor picks up the puppy, heads out behind the booth, and comes back with the dead puppy in a bag for his customer to take with her. Naturally, the nurse was horrified, and as I recall, she started throwing up. That's how I feel whenever anyone around me orders beef, or chicken, or fish—I feel like throwing up. But freewill is freewill, and I'm NOT going to give a lecture here, or try and convert anyone to vegetarianism—but I do have two questions:

Question #1: Why is a dog's life or a cat's life worth more than the life of a cow or a chicken? I don't see it. It's been proven that animals have feelings and are social beings; and I just saw a documentary where scientists are now saying that our DNA is not that much different from that of the animals we eat.

Question #2: When people find out I'm vegetarian, or when I'm out to dinner with a non-vegetarian, why do they feel the need to apologize to me for eating meat? If they really felt that eating animals was okay, there would be no need for an apology!

I think that most people, upon spending 5 minutes in a slaughterhouse, would immediately convert to vegetarianism. I also think that with so many meat alternatives out there, they could convert with very little distress. There! I've said my piece! That is all the lecturing you will hear from me about being a vegetarian in this book!

Evolution & Entities who are different from the "norm"

"Human beings are a myriad of emotions. We are this way for a reason. We are all here to feel and to experience things, and for that purpose we need our senses and our emotions. Some people seem to be ultra sensitive and we say that these people are the ones who are more awake and more spiritual.

People who think about other's feelings and who think about the feelings of lesser life forms on the planet are really move evolved and awake than those who do not. Think about the level of evolution it takes on the part of a human being to eschew the hunting and eating of animals. It is not an easy thing to be 'overly' sensitive, and it is not an easy thing to be the lone vegetarian in a family or circle of friends. One of the most difficult ways to be different, though, is to be gay or lesbian.

It is not easy to be different on the planet Earth, but there is a reason for that and it is so there is an atmosphere and environment that allows you to step out and apart from the crowd. If all were the same, how could you make a statement or have experiences to help you move along in your development? Those who choose to be different are pioneers in the very real sense of the word."

I have been overly emotional my entire life. I cry at the movies and even at some of the commercials that are on TV! I cry at sad stories and at happy stories. I can't help myself. It's embarrassing, and while being a little sensitive or even overly sensitive can be a pain in the neck, and listening to all the cracks about being vegetarian is annoying, these things are *nothing* compared to the pain that those who have chosen to be gay are forced to endure. Two very close friends of mine during this incarnation happen to be lesbians, and when the Guides mentioned that those who are different are often pioneers, I immediately felt the truth of that statement. I see what my friends go through, starting with the insensitivity of those around, and all the way up to the fact that they don't have many of the same basic rights that heterosexuals enjoy. Things are obviously changing, progress is being made, and thanks to some very brave souls—some states now recognize gay marriage and some employers now provide benefits to life partners. I don't know for sure, but I doubt that was the case 20 years ago. I think you have to be made of very strong stuff to enter this world as a gay man or as a lesbian—I don't think I could handle it. I take a lot of verbal abuse for being a yoga-practicing, new-age vegetarian, but I can still marry whomever I choose and put him on my health insurance. The GG went on to finish this section with the following...

> *"The souls who choose to incarnate with a disability such as a major disease or who are deaf or blind or something that is disfiguring—they are very brave souls who truly love their soul groups because they are putting themselves out there for a very difficult life in that incarnation. People make fun of you in front of your face and behind your back—you can never do the things everyone else is capable of doing or even try to do them. You can't go to regular school or you don't fit in. You miss out on most of the good stuff that comes with being incarnated on this planet. It's not all dreary lessons, you know, being incarnated is also fun experiences, too.*
>
> *So far as relationship villains go when it comes to disabilities; well, are there really villains involved? There are those who learn, and perhaps the relationship villain who makes fun of a disabled person is one who sets the stage for others to learn or to step up and follow a path they might otherwise have missed, or go through a window of opportunity they might not have noticed. Perhaps the relationship villain in these cases is really the one who sets everything in place and makes it happen. It could be that outside of the incarnation, the villain and the victim are actually the closest of friends—entities working together in different ways for the good of others. Do you see?"*

These two paragraphs serve as a good reminder that we should be careful about judging others as we open our eyes to look for windows of opportunity.

Evolution: Some things to think about

- Humankind is evolving as a species not just spiritually, but in body too.

- Generations of children called Indigo, Crystal, and Rainbow, are here now to help us evolve and raise the vibrational level of the planet. Each new group arrives as the vibrational levels of the planet change to accommodate their specific energy.

- Lightworkers are those individuals who are on the front line for change, like "flower children," civil rights activists, equal rights activists, and those who are perceived as "different," like those who are gay, lesbian, and even vegetarian.

- Lightworkers help to raise the vibrational level of the planet by raising their own levels and being an inspiration for change to those around them.

- 2012 is the end of the Mayan Calendar. Changes predicted for 2012 have been taking place for a long time. There will be a certain amount of upheaval, but humankind can keep that upheaval to a minimum by collectively raising their vibrational levels which will in turn raise the levels of our planet. Increased levels equal an easier shift.

- We can all help to bring light to the planet and raise the vibrational level by increasing our output of positive energy, decreasing our output of negative energy, and by following the Golden Rule and being nice to each other.

- The planet Earth will eventually experience peace and its inhabitants will be free from Karmic cycle, as we become more aware of our connection to the Source, and of our interconnection with each other.

CHAPTER SIX
Learning & Growth

Life changes

The Group wants us to understand that people must change in order to evolve, and that the very act of evolving forces changes in our behavior and our outlook regarding our surroundings. And it affects our planet. Often when one begins to wake up and starts changing the way he/she looks at things or does things, it is upsetting to those *around* the evolving entity. People change jobs and often even change friends as they go through life, and the Guides want us to understand that this is not a bad thing and we shouldn't feel hurt if it happens to us. Instead we should examine the circumstances and look for windows of opportunity for growth and learning.

"What happens when someone suddenly changes the way they are or the way they act, or the things they are interested in? These are signs that growth has happened or is taking place. When people put aside things they once loved, it doesn't mean that something is wrong, it just means that other interests are taking their place and their time with those things is past. There is nothing more to learn from it and it is taking time away from other interests that must be pursued in order to continue with their growth cycle on this planet. We should not judge others when someone changes something or puts something aside; instead the change should be supported by those entities around them."

I mentioned earlier that three members of the Guide Group are my relatives who have passed over, and from the other side, each of them keeps a watchful and protective eye on their family members still on this side of the veil. I get a little break in the next section as the Group switches from me to my sisters to help make their point.

> *" Let's look at your sister, Debbie, and how she is growing now at an accelerated rate. She is waking up and stretching out her arms! She was stagnant for a long time but now pursues various interests and is becoming an independent woman. These are big changes for her, but would she have been able to accomplish them if she had stayed in California? Of course not. She had to leave and there were some who would judge her harshly, her children included, for making the changes that brought her back to New York and to a new life. She had to do what she did in order for her to grow and to continue on her path. She had to think of herself at that point—do you see what we are saying?"*

My sister, Debbie Smith, married young and moved to California in the late 70s with her husband, whose father had relocated there a few years earlier. No doubt they were very much in love, but drugs and alcohol took their toll on the relationship and it turned abusive. Debbie waited until her children were grown and then found the strength to leave this abusive relationship and move back to New York to be near family. She worked full time while putting herself through school to qualify for better job opportunities. Based on the insight provided by the Group, it seems obvious that Debbie had to think of herself and move on in order for her to grow, yet people did and may still judge her for leaving her kids in California. They were older, 16 and 18, and chose to stay in California, even though they could have moved east with their mother. It was a very difficult decision she had to make to move away from them in order to continue on her path.

> *"Your sister, Kathy, and her husband are on the brink of a great change right now. Kathy will flourish as she has never flourished before because she is about to take major steps in her growth as a human being. First she will take steps to open herself up to new activities and opportunities from which she will learn, grow and touch other people."*

Shortly after this was dictated, Kathy's husband, George Seeley, had a quadruple by-pass, and a few months later was diagnosed with inoperable lung cancer, forcing them both into a time of great change. He passed over recently, and Kathy is embarking on her new path, which is scary, but necessary for her continued growth.

> *"Those who stay stagnant are usually in a period of stunted growth and that's the fact of the matter. They are in a state of non-movement and they have to find the strength to move. Things are only natural if you are in a state of constant change. If you look at your own life, you will see that you live in five-year cycles—almost everything in your life changes every five years and lately it has been three-year cycles and that will accelerate shortly. That is the growth pattern of a human being—to grow and to change! To stay stagnant is to impede growth and that, my dear, is the last thing a human being wants to do, especially one who is awake!"*

So much for giving me a break! Looking back to the 80s I can recognize distinct and clear-cut, five-year cycles in my life. Starting in 2000, I noticed things were speeding up and I can clearly recognize three-year cycles. In fact, the completion of this book will be the end of a cycle for me. I think I'm starting one-year cycles now and I feel like I'm on a roller coaster!

Life changes: why and when they happen

"Let's talk about the choices people make for themselves even when they sometimes adversely affect those around them. The bottom line here is that we are each responsible for ourselves and for our own growth. That is our primary task and our primary responsibility on this planet.

Those around us, with whom we have chosen to incarnate, are here to help us as we are here to help them. Those are the various roles we play. The fact is that we are many things to many people. To some we are the nicest person in the world, to others we are a pain in the neck neighbor! We have roles as loving mothers, fathers, daughters, sons, brothers, sisters, friends, bosses, employees, and co-workers. So many different relationships, but all with one thing in common, they were all planned from the start. None are accidents.

There are no coincidences—we plan our lives at a planning table where we sit and decide what it is we want to accomplish in this incarnation. And so too, sometimes people who seem like they are our enemies or are bad people while we are in body, could be the best friend you'll ever know because they have taken on the extra additional responsibility of being the bad guy. This is the 'relationship villain' that we have spoken about

114

before. It takes someone who really loves you to be the bad guy—anyone can play the good guy in these little earthly dramas that we call our lives! Now let's talk about these dramas we live through as each life cycle is like a soap opera with many different actors coming in and out and the main characters staying the same.

The dramas we live through can be downsized and they can be ended. In doing so, we progress more quickly and make our lives easier and we can better enjoy our time on this earth. How can we do this? We can look for and recognize windows of opportunity that pop up. So how do you recognize them? Here are some things to consider: **Is the same type of event occurring in your life?**

If so, it could be that you are continually abused, either verbally or physically, in relationships. Your relationships could be part of a life script where you continue to attract the same type of person as a husband, wife, friend, or boss; or the abuser could be someone in your family. If so, this is probably something you co-created for yourself before you came into this body and those who are doing the abusing are carrying out your orders. But if you take action and put a stop to it, if you refuse to accept the abusive behavior anymore, then you WILL put a stop to it. But you must be strong, and you must stand up for yourself and say, 'NO! NO MORE!' And then you must take the steps to make it stop even if it means leaving or ending a relationship.

These are situations we set up for ourselves so that we can learn and grow. At the time we are doing the planning, we know what lesson we want to learn and we are confident that we will see the window and quickly go through it. But the veil is hiding the window of opportunity and the shade is down when we get to this side—it's not as easy as we thought it would be. We do set up difficult situations for ourselves, but we never intend to stay in them forever! We have to exercise freewill and take control of our lives.

Relationships are not meant to last for the entire lifetime of an individual on Earth.

Some do, of course. The relationship with your parents and siblings, and other close relatives—those are usually your core group of souls that incarnate together to support each other. But friends, co-workers, neighbors, acquaintances, they usually come and go in order to serve you and for you to serve them.

We tell you again that it is not a bad thing, rather it is a good thing to have many acquaintances come and go. It means that you are not stagnating—you are making progress. It is when we get bogged down and continue relationships even when they are painful or unrewarding that we stagnate ourselves, and it is at precisely those times that we should be looking for life scripts or windows. Check to see if you are living the same thing over and over again with different people under different circumstances. If you are, analyze the situation and take action so you can move forward."

As I mentioned earlier, I've had friends come and go throughout my life. Some friendships ended with a bang, some just ended. I've had friendships just stop, with no real explanation or reason why, and then start-up again years later. I've ended friendships and I've had people end friendships with me. I'm sure I'm not alone in these experiences. Sometimes we get hurt, and sometimes we hurt others. Sometimes there is no hurt, you just wake up years later and wonder "whatever happened to [insert name here] and why aren't we friends anymore?" Now we know—people grow and change—and we need different people in our lives at different times. It's okay for friendships to end! But what about when a friendship that seemingly ended starts up again? What does that mean?

In the last couple of years, I've re-connected with three people I was very close to for many years, and our friendships just kind of fizzled, probably due to the fact that I moved to Florida, and they got married and had kids to raise. Two of these friendships (Debbie Silvestri Amico and Peggy Jetter McGrath) began in elementary school and just kind of ended in our thirties after I moved. When I reconnected with Debbie, she was going through a divorce. I didn't know this when I called her after 16 years of zero contact; I just had an overwhelming mental push to make the call. After a decade and a half of no contact, I was suddenly aware of commercials and TV shows about the King Tut exhibit, and King Tut in general. Debbie and I went to the first King Tut exhibit at the MET in New York City in the late 70s. Every time I saw a King Tut commercial, I thought about Debbie and finally I called her, after 16 years! She told me she had been thinking about me too! Coincidence? I doubt it. Synchronicity? I think so. No one sees that many commercials and advertisements for the same subject over and over again without a reason—that kind of thing is a message from your guides, your angels, or your higher-self. Sometimes from all three, depending on how long it takes you to get the message!

My friendship with Linda Conklin started in high school and continued uninterrupted until we were in our early 40s. I remember making a conscious decision to pull back for awhile because I didn't like her new husband one bit, I didn't like the way he treated her or her kids, and I felt that if I opened my mouth, our friendship would suffer. We didn't speak for several years, and then one night she called to tell me she was getting a divorce! As she talked about what happened, it turned out that her ex-husband was a "Jim clone" and we provided a lot of therapy and support for each other! Debbie and Linda are two people that I would seek out in times of trouble, no matter how many years had passed, so I'm not surprised that we re-bonded during difficult life challenges. Peggy didn't have anything traumatic going on when we got back together and I didn't either—it looks like we reconnected for the fun of it, and it *is* fun reminiscing with people you have a shared history with!

I've noticed, too, that I have several friends that I rarely get to spend time with, but when I do see them, it's like we've never been apart. That's how it is for me with my friends Denise Shelby Isseks, and Marie Mauro Hansen. I met Denise when I was 15, and Marie when I was 17—I'm 51 as this book goes to press, so we've been friends a very long time. We may be separated by geography, children, and life in general, but like Debbie, Linda and Peggy, when we speak on the phone or get together, it's as if no time has passed—we pick up right where we left off, and I really treasure the time I have with them. I asked the GG about this and here's what they said:

> *"Friends like this are earth angels for each other, and these entities have known each other from the beginning of time and experienced multiple lifetimes together. There is a psychic connection between such entities. They are like fail safes for each other as they can always seek each other out for counseling."*

Remember, if you start seeing or hearing the same thing over and over, it's probably a message from the other side—when you notice it, pay attention to what you're seeing and hearing, and take action. Paying attention to these messages has helped me reconnect with many people and my life is better for it.

Life Changes—you can make them happen

> *"Do you have the same unpleasant things happen over and over?* For instance, do people always seem to cut you off in traffic or bump into you in grocery stores? Maybe you need to look at the way you deal with these situations and change it. Then they will stop! Not only can you make unpleasant things less unpleasant or stop them altogether, you can make good things happen for yourself. Karma and the windows of opportunity you've planned for yourself not withstanding, you do have freewill and you know that thoughts are things. So use your thoughts, use that positive energy to create pleasant circumstances for yourself. If you dwell on the negative you will draw negativity to you—that is the Law of Attraction [Karma]! If you expect the best in situations, the best will happen. The situations we plan for ourselves have degrees of difficulty attached to them. Think negatively and the task will be harder, think positively and the task will be easier to handle. It sounds simple but it is another one of those truths that is easier to say than to do."*

Remember that road rage I told you about earlier? When I recognized it and made a decision to end it, a lot less people were pulling out in front of me—with their cars *and* with their grocery carts. I used to lose my temper whenever anyone pulled out in front of me or bumped into me, and while I'm not entirely sure why I felt this way; I'm pretty sure I looked at those kinds of things as signs of disrespect towards me. Once I decided to calm down and not turn a molehill into a mountain (really—these people didn't even know me, how could they be disrespecting me?), things changed almost immediately. Now when someone pulls out in front of me, I smile and wave, and in return I usually get a "thank you" or an apology because they pulled out so suddenly.

The second part of what the GG dictated above reminds me of "The Secret." I think the information in that book has been around for a long time, but the way the information is packaged is great, and I've quoted from that book many times. In fact, I bought copies of the DVD for my Mother and both of my sisters, and I've given away so many copies of the book to friends and acquaintances, you'd think I was making a commission on it! Last year, an acquaintance of mine went through a very unpleasant divorce and began a relationship that she knew wasn't right for her. And as she dated the wrong guy, she was wishing for the right guy to come along. She and I had a long discussion and I told her I had read a story in "The Secret" about a woman who wanted to meet someone special but was having no luck. To help attract a relationship, she made room in her closet for "his" clothes and left room in the garage for "his" car. In short, she behaved like "he" was already there! And then she met him! I suggested to my friend that if she ended the relationship she knew was wrong for her, she would have room in her life for "the one." Within days of breaking off the relationship she met her fiancé!

Accidents are *not* accidental

Before you begin this section, it is important that you understand that this applies to what we on this side of the veil view as "accidents," the GG are not talking about homicide or suicide. After my friend, Leigh Herr, read this section, she told me she wanted to know more about how the following information applies to murder, and that prompted me to go back to the GG to ask for more information, which will be covered later in this section. The GG were very clear that this section is about *planned* **accidents**.

"Let us talk about what happens when human beings appear to have had an accident. There are no accidents of this nature. These things are all planned ahead of time. Accidents are pre-planned events designed as very big windows of opportunity for people to learn from. Now here's the interesting part: The person who suffers the most is not necessarily a victim, but someone who is so loving and kind that they have agreed to make a big sacrifice so that others around them will have a window or windows of opportunity from which to learn. Do you see what we are saying? And the person who causes the accident is not necessarily the bad guy—it may well be that the 'villain' is also someone who cares enough to play that role so that those involved can have opportunities to learn and grow. It may also be Karma that causes a group of souls to be involved in or to be part of an accident together. There may be a debt to be paid, or it could be that one or more of the parties involved has decided that this is the best way for them to learn and advance to the next level. Again, though, the window is created by the accident and how people react after it happens is vitally important—the handling of the situation is of the utmost importance for the learning and growth to take place.

Let us talk more about accidents and the nature of them. What are the odds of two people or more ending up in exactly the right place at the right time to make an accident happen? It comes from very careful planning—careful orchestration of entire lives. So that is why there are no coincidences. Everything, every part of a person's life has to be planned or how can these things happen?

When we say every detail, there are certainly the windows of opportunity, but there is also freewill. Even though a window is planned, we are free to walk through it or to ignore it. We hope, no we EXPECT, as we are planning, that we will recognize and go through the windows. It's never as easy as we think it will be when we are making our plans!"

I asked the Group about my nephew, who was involved in several car accidents in a very short period of time. It seemed like he had a car accident or some kind of incident with his car every few weeks—it was even stolen one night from his apartment complex!

"If ever there was an entity that wants to learn a lesson, it is he. He continues to attract the same circumstances to himself in order to learn, but has yet to step up to the plate and follow through. Right now he blames it all on bad luck, but he is nearing the time when he will wake up and all this will stop. But ask yourself how many accidents can one person have and how much bad luck can one person have? Well the truth is, as many and as much as it takes! And this one has prepared himself well to continue to have these windows pop up for himself until he recognizes what he needs to see and moves on. Then he will say his luck has changed!"

My nephew's "luck" did change and it seemed to happen overnight! He stopped having car accidents and car incidents, and became an amazingly responsible person. As he was nearing the end of that cycle (although we didn't know then that it was almost over), we had a conversation where he told me that even though he wanted to change things about his life, he kept migrating to the same types of people and the same types of situations. He was recognizing a pattern and looking for a way to end it! That's how you go through a window of opportunity! I can tell you that my nephew now has a very responsible management position, is happily married with two children, and recently bought his first house! Once he recognized that window and walked through it, things changed for him very quickly.

Accidents open multiple windows of opportunity

"An accident doesn't just affect the victim, it affects his family, his friends, his employer—all the lives he touches at the hospital, the drug store, the doctor's office, everywhere he goes he affects and touches people's lives. We just don't realize what's going on because we are not awake. But you can know that this is a fact: accidents are the things that are the most non-accidental in the universe! Accidents are the things that are the most planned and talked about, because those accidents must happen for the wheels of Karma to turn, for windows of opportunity to open, and for freewill to be exercised by a multitude of human beings.

Accidents are like markers in our lives that are the points from which so many windows of opportunities open, and those who think that they are coincidences are asleep and snoring! So the bottom line is that many wheels are in motion to get the participants to planned places at the planned times.

There are no coincidences and there are no accidents. Only pre-planned events and the pre-planned windows that each event causes in the lives of those touched. Do you see how far reaching an accident can be?

As we begin to wake up, we start to see the far-reaching effects that an accident has on the lives of many people. Those who are intimately involved, the victim, the one who caused the accident, their families, their employers, their co-workers, their friends—so many people are touched by a single accident.

Let us talk now about the devastating, paralyzing, life-changing type of accident—not the fender benders. Fender benders are annoying and provide windows of freewill/opportunity for all involved, but are not on the same level as a big accident like the type your parents were involved in. Major accidents provide us with opportunities to react in a myriad of different ways:

- *Some react with sadness.*
- *Some are in shock.*
- *Some stagnate, while some deal with it and move on.*
- *Some become caregivers (possibly allowing them to complete a Karmic cycle).*
- *Some refuse to become caregivers and turn their backs on those in need.*
- *Some continue to be friends or to be close to the "victim."*
- *Some move way from the "victim."*

All of these reactions are possible and important to the "players" in any particular accident. They are all ways for the individuals involved to learn and grow and provide additional windows of opportunity to others around them. Accidents are very far-reaching and provide so many windows of opportunities for so many people. This concept is so important that we must continue to elaborate on it. Accidents have far-reaching, rippling effects, and for that reason you should be able to see that these things cannot be coincidences.

Accidents themselves are carefully planned, and again the relationship villain here is the one who causes the accident to happen. That person is doing something that was planned by the entities collectively, and the so-called 'villain' is doing the job that he or she signed on to do so that all the others can have the learning experiences and windows of opportunity that will be created by that one single accident. This is why we must learn to look at all sides of an accident and realize that there is more to it than meets the eye. If we do that then we can learn the lesson and not keep attracting similar experiences to ourselves."

To help me comprehend this information, the Group chose to highlight a car accident my parents were involved in when I was very young. My father was driving, and another woman, a friend of my parents, died as a result of the accident. The Group told me that this woman's death provided multiple windows of opportunity for many different entities, and the woman who died, agreed to pass over at that time so that her family and friends would have opportunities for growth. They were very clear that she was not a victim, but someone who cared so much for the others involved that she wanted to make this sacrifice for them.

Even before learning about windows of opportunity through this dictated material from the GG, I felt deep down that this accident my parents were involved in was a turning point of some sort, I just didn't understand how or why. I wish that this information about accidents was known back in the 60s —I think many of those involved, particularly my Father, would have suffered much less had they understood the true nature of accidents. There is no way that I can know if the windows that were opened that night were utilized, and I wouldn't presume to judge him or anyone else involved in that accident, but I do feel that there is still pain and guilt that goes on to this day because of it, and that accident happened many decades ago. When I first starting receiving the notes on this subject, I didn't want to include them in the book because I felt it would seem as if the Group was minimizing the pain and anguish we experience from accidents. As I worked on this chapter, and was forced to confront and analyze the pain of just one single car accident that heavily impacted so many in my family, I changed my mind. Working on this section forced me to recognize that healing and opportunity will come to many people who will now have a better understanding of the nature of accidents. That's why the Group dictated the notes about it, and that's why I'm passing this information on now—so that anyone who finds themselves in the same heart-wrenching circumstances that my family did will be able to forgive themselves, heal, and recognize and go through the windows of opportunity attached to the tragedy.

Murder

As I mentioned earlier, my friend Leigh wanted to know more about murder and how that fit into the planning of a lifetime. I understood why she wanted more information on this subject, she had personally experienced the murder of a family member, and so I asked the GG if they could provide some insight. As you will see, they had a lot to say on this subject.

> *"Murder is a nasty business and generally-speaking, murder is not a planned experience. It is usually an accident or some aberration of freewill where a soul goes too far in expressing his or her anger. Our understanding of murder is that it is a tragic occurrence that tests the souls involved to the maximum degree.*
>
> *People react in different ways to murder and the experience will absolutely test their faith in their beliefs, in themselves, and in those around them, as they go through the grieving process, but murder is not something that is planned prior to an incarnation. This does not speak to war—war is a different scenario where death on the battlefield is in service of one's country—that is preplanned and is an example of group Karma. Killing in a war is different than pre-meditated murder, or murder as a crime of passion.*
>
> *Again we say that murder is an aberration, and let us speak now of those who commit murder. They are souls who have suffered a dysfunction of their circuits, so to speak. No one sets out to be a murderer and no one plans to be murdered—it just isn't done. So where does this aberration or dysfunction come from and how does it start? It often starts when a soul finds itself in a situation or series of situations that is simply too much for it to handle.*
>
> *Often souls wish to be extremely aggressive in their life plan. Their Guides and those on their planning committee will attempt to intercede and sometimes they win and sometimes they do*

not—freewill isn't something that exists only on your side of the veil. When a soul goes ahead and plunges into circumstances they are not strong enough to handle, the brain can short-circuit. Incarnating souls choose the parents and the environments that will help them accomplish their goals, and sometimes, a soul, in its desire to progress quickly, will put themselves in situations they are not strong enough to handle.

Short circuits generally happen early in life. Early childhood development is crucial, and when a soul is ill-treated as a child, the shock the soul experiences is like a fuse that burns out. Sometimes it takes only one incident and sometimes it takes several. This is also the cause of what is referred to as split personalities, where the soul splinters in an attempt to protect itself.

Let us speak now of murder when it is a crime of passion. This is not pre-meditated and it is not generally brought about by the mistreatment of a soul at an early age. This type of murder is a temporary short circuit, and is something that the soul deeply regrets and is unprepared to deal with. This is an emotional act and much pain is caused when a plan of learning and growth is cut short because of one tragic moment."

As I took the dictation for this section, and having already learned how carefully we plan our lives, I wondered what happened to those plans, and especially what happens to the lives of those affected by a murder. It wasn't long before the GG supplied information to answer my question . . .

So what of the rest of the life of the person who commits murder? What of the lives of other souls whose incarnations and life plans have been interrupted because of this act? What of all the carefully constructed windows of opportunity that will never open and those carefully planned experiences, painstakingly put together that will never take place because of this act?

Well, new plans must be made. Old plans altered. How is this accomplished? Changes are organized by the Higher Self! The Higher Self is in communication with the part of itself that is the incarnated soul, and together with the soul's Guides, and the presence of others on the other side of the veil who are necessary for re-planning, an emergency planning session is called to order. A life, an incarnation, cannot be wasted. New plans are set into action to accomplish goals, new contacts are made and new plans are made through the Higher Self on the other side of the veil. The Higher Self operates on both sides of the veil, and is able to make adjustments when unforeseen circumstances occur. New windows of opportunity are formed and goals are altered or changed in order to make the most of a bad situation. We wish to add here that the Higher Self is very aware of what is happening during an incarnation and sometimes is able to do a bit of cosmic surgery and make adjustments before too much or any of the life plan is altered. That is how someone who was cruel when young can grow up to be a nice person.

Murder is a sad occurrence and it changes the balance and life plan for many souls. So much must be re-shuffled, and that happens as an emergency care network is formed on our side of the veil. The situation is carefully evaluated and strategic planning takes place as new windows are created based on the new situations of all whose lives have been disrupted. For the one who is incarcerated, there are still opportunities for growth, and if the soul is damaged irrevocably, that is where the soul should stay so it does not hurt others and cause more damage to intricate life plans. Because so many are involved, a change of plans on this level requires many to fix it and create the new action plans. For those who are related to, friends with, or romantically involved with the soul who commits murder, it is a shock for them, and while their original life plan will be altered, such a thing provides opportunities for them to learn and grow. All must make the best out of a tragic situation."

During the time period this section was being dictated, I happened to catch part of a show on TV about Jeffrey Dahmer, and other serial murderers. They all looked so normal, but it was said on the show that they had all suffered during their childhoods, and they showed similar signs of trouble to come, like torturing and killing small animals. I didn't think it was a coincidence that I found this show while I was channel-surfing, and the next day, the GG dictated the following:

"We know that your attention has turned to serial killers and mass murderers, and again, this is an example of an aberration in the circuitry that could not be fixed. Serial killers are not planned for and set forth upon the world. Ted Bundy, Jeffrey Dahmer, and Adolph Hitler did not sit at planning tables making plans with those they would eventually murder. So what happens to serial killers and mass murderers like Jim Jones?

Are they greeted with open arms when they come home? Of course they are—they are children of God as we are all children of God. These children have gone very much off course, that is obvious, and they must be helped. You have a saying on your side of the veil that 'no child is left behind.' On this side, no soul is left behind. The souls who commit these heinous acts are greeted, counseled, then put into a type of sleep mode, because when they arrive here, they are appalled and shocked by what they have done. They require a long period of rest and lengthy (decades of) counseling.

Remember, these are souls who were abused and suffered, and consequently their circuits went haywire. It is important to know that when this happens, these souls are eventually stopped, although not as quickly as we would all like. As we have said before, the Higher Self knows that something has gone wrong, and the rescue squad is working to help the Higher Self put a stop to the aberration. As they are creating new windows to adjust for what is going on, they are creating windows that will allow the murderer to be caught and stopped."

I can understand that someone like Jeffrey Dahmer or Jim Jones had a screw loose, but Adolph Hitler? The Holocaust was mass murder on a pretty big scale, and for Hitler to be put into a coma followed by intensive counseling hardly seems plausible. I asked the GG for more information about Hitler and they explained that many windows of opportunity were created to stop it first from happening at all, and later to end it quickly. Those who could make a difference didn't act at all, or didn't act soon enough, and the GG insists that there was a glitch in the collective consciousness of many individual souls who were caught up in an unprecedented state of group fear. Fear kept people from taking action individually and as a group. I guess this explanation makes sense, but apparently I am not as evolved as I would like to think because I still think Hitler got off easy. This is a subject that I intend to meditate on and learn more about.

Suicide

"The subject of suicide is similar to murder, yet different. Those poor souls who commit suicide are instantly sorry they did so. We've said this before and we will say it again: the planning that goes into a life plan is very intricate, very involved, and to cut short that life because one is overwhelmed and feels unable to complete an incarnation, is a very sad situation. Many times entities take on too much against the advice of their teachers and mentors, and the pressure is so great that they become 'soul sick' and long for home. Longing for home may not be what the soul is consciously aware of, they may simply want to end the pain and don't know what else to do. But they are soul sick and they long for the comfort of home. Or, they want to punish someone and think attempting suicide will help make their point. We say 'attempt' here because souls who wish to punish or make others feel badly through this act rarely intend to 'go all the way.' Their intent is to scare people into changing their behavior or make them feel badly.

Suicide not only ends an incarnation, it ends an important opportunity to learn and grow. An opportunity to incarnate is a precious gift. There are more souls than opportunities to incarnate,

132

and when you consider the time it takes to find just the right circumstances—the right parents, location, etc., it is mind-boggling to us to think about, and incomprehensible on your side of the veil. And please remember that each incarnation takes us closer to our ultimate goal, which is to NOT have to come back. For these reasons suicide is very sad.

Suicide is an indicator that an entity has taken on too much, or changes have occurred that the soul was unable or unprepared to deal with. When a person takes his own life, it is an unplanned event and the same rescue squad that we discussed when we spoke about murder jumps into action. The difference here is that they are working with a soul who suddenly finds itself on the other side of the veil and is quite surprised by it. And now the soul is upset and remorseful because he realizes what personal opportunities he has given up, and he feels guilt about the situations and windows he was to be part of for others that now cannot take place. Again, we see much clearer here on this side, and the soul who has committed suicide understands the tremendous amount of work that now must take place to re-design and place new windows of opportunity. He knows he did not live up to his contract and did not fulfill his obligation to his soul group. This soul will undergo a great deal of counseling to help him be prepared for his next incarnation. Those who step in to counsel will not judge, but will help the soul to be better prepared in the future. Suicide is a sorrowful occurrence for all who are affected."

While visiting with my good friends Fred and Debbie Lowman, I mentioned that I was working on a section about suicide for this book. I was very surprised when Fred told me that a good friend of his had committed suicide. Fred's friend, Ken, was 41 when he took his own life, and it appears that he put a lot of thought into hurting the people he felt were responsible for his pain. As Fred tells the story, Ken brought Fred over a stack of his T-shirts, and days later shot himself on his ex-wife's birthday, while on the telephone with his ex-girlfriend. Why did he do it? Financial trouble brought on by his ex-girlfriend. Ken couldn't keep his business up because he sold all of the inventory and gave the money to his girlfriend. He even cashed in a life insurance policy with a death benefit of $200,000 for just $10,000 in cash and gave that money to his girlfriend, too. And when all of Ken's money was gone, and he couldn't get anymore, his girlfriend dumped him. Fred says that Ken was very talented and could have turned his business and his life around, but it appears that Ken was out to hurt those he felt hurt him—his ex-wife and his ex-girlfriend. I know Ken's action had a deep affect on Fred, who, after many years still says, "I can't believe he did that to me." This is such a heart-breaking story, and I can't help but notice how it seems to fit into what the GG had to say about this very sad subject.

Responsibility To Your Family

"Today we are talking about the responsibilities people have to their families. The fact of the matter is that people often feel they must stick around to protect or help others in their family, and so they suppress their own wants and desires to do this.

There is always another way if you look for it. People must learn to think about themselves first, take care of themselves first, and everything else will fall into place. When people give up what they want to achieve to take care of or to help others, then it creates a Karmic debt that doesn't have to be. This can lead in some instances to making the other person, the person they care so much about, feel guilty or less empowered.

Now the truth is that there are some situations where an entity has agreed to be part of a relationship where someone is or becomes handicapped, and if you look at families like this, you will see the majority of handicapped people forge ahead, doing things and living life as much like so called 'normal people' as they possibly can. And so do their families!

It is in those relationships where families, or one or two members of a family, make taking care of that person exclusive to their lives that the trouble begins.

When people sacrifice themselves 100% for others, they think they are doing the noble and right thing, but they are actually causing more harm than good. You must make people understand that it is not wrong or selfish to think about themselves first. It gives others the opportunity to think about themselves and take responsibility for themselves. It gives everyone the chance to be a whole human being and get the most out of the experience."

At this point, the Group used Christopher Reeves and his wife, Dana, as an example of how to take care of those we care about, while still taking care of ourselves. This section was dictated more than a year before Dana Reeves death from lung cancer in March 2006:

> *"Christopher Reeves' wife certainly stuck by his side and takes care of him, but she is also involved in fundraising causes and has a life of her own. Christopher didn't sit around feeling sorry for himself either. He embraced the handicap and went forward, neither one giving up who they were, just adding to who they were, and using 'tragedy' to help themselves and others."*

My family has not faced anything on the level of what happened to Christopher and Dana Reeves, but my sister did spend nearly a year taking care of her husband when he was dying of cancer. And my Aunts, Sandra Knapp and Janet Collins, have faced having to care for and make difficult decisions regarding the care of elderly members of my family; first my Grandmother and then my Grandmother's sister, Viola. I can remember when they made the hard choice to put Aunt Viola into a nursing home. It was extremely emotional and hard to do, but the Group has shared with me that it was the right thing to do. Had Sandra and Janet continued to keep Viola at home, they would have been forced into the role of caretaker virtually 24 hours a day and would have no time for their own lives. I have it on good authority (the GG) that it would have stagnated *their* own growth and it wouldn't have helped Viola to recover had she remained at home.

This section was very interesting to me—It's almost as if in addition to relationship villains, there are also "relationship martyrs" who sacrifice themselves for the sake of helping others. At one time I would have thought they were like angels on Earth, but now, if I understand this section correctly, we must allow others to take responsibility for themselves and not put our own lives on hold to help other people. Not that we can't assist, but we shouldn't smother them with help to the exclusion of taking care of ourselves and our own needs.

Learning & Growth: Some things to think about

- Change is natural and necessary for evolution, for ourselves and for our planet. Continual change is an indicator of progress.

- Losing touch with friends and acquaintances is a normal part of life.

- We should support, instead of judge, when people we know change in ways we may not understand.

- We all play different roles in each other's lives, and we can avoid excess drama and pain by recognizing windows of opportunity as they occur. Those involved must evaluate the situation from their individual perspective and decide how to handle the situation; i.e. recognizing windows of opportunity and going through them.

- What we perceive to be accidents are pre-planned events set in motion for growth and learning. Accidents provide multiple windows of opportunity for many souls.

- Murder and Suicide are not pre-planned events. They are caused by a type of short-circuit in the brain and action must be taken to re-plan windows of opportunity cut short by these acts.

CHAPTER SEVEN
Extraterrestrials

The GG have made several references to beings from other planets, and I asked them to elaborate on who they are and why they are here.

"Today let's turn our attention to UFOs and visitors from other planets. This is not such a strange topic because many believe that there are now, and have been visitors from other planets throughout Earth's history. The truth is that people from other planets have always been involved in our history. Sometimes they watch from the side lines and sometimes they are actively involved. We have it on good authority that representatives from other planets are on and around the Earth now to make sure that the planet is not blown up by the human race. A nuclear holocaust would upset the structure of our universe and our galaxy. It appears that human beings are not 100% trusted to protect the planet; therefore, there are watchers from other planets to keep things under control. Another reason for the visitors to be here is that they are working in conjunction with the Lightworkers on the planet, and with representatives from several planets who are currently stationed above the planet, to help bring enough light to Earth to make the 2012 shift as painless as possible.

Even though visitors have been part of Earth history since the beginning of time, in recent Earth history, sightings began again in the 1940s and 1950s, especially during the time of nuclear bomb testing. It is our understanding that world governments are aware of the presence of the watchers and they choose to keep their citizens in ignorance.

There are several different groups of beings presently here who are interested in the continued development and safety of planet Earth. The main contingents are from the Pleiades and Arcturus, although other planets are represented as well.

Freewill and what we do with it is a large part of the curriculum on schoolhouse Earth, and the watchers must allow us our freewill. However, they are under orders to stop us from blowing ourselves up. Those orders come directly from the High Council. There is a High Council of highly elevated beings whose word is law and who govern the universe."

I've seen references to the "Great White Brotherhood" in almost every channeled book I've ever read, but the "High Council" was a term I wasn't familiar with. I did some research on the internet, and found many sites with lots of information. I thought Lightworker and Healer David Raphael Issacson's explanation of the Great White Brotherhood on his "Merlin's Magical Mystery School," website was particularly thorough, interesting, and easy to understand. Here's a brief paraphrased explanation from that website:

"The High Council is part of the Great White Brotherhood. The Great White Brotherhood is made up of ascended masters (Jesus is included), and entities from various planets, dimensions, and levels of consciousness. The High Council is an arm of the Great White Brotherhood that coordinates and plans detailed operations that involve all the inhabitants of entire worlds and universes."

When I read the information on the website, it made me think about what the GG said about 2012 and the need to usher in as much light as possible to minimize the effects of the expected shift of our planet. Someone needs to be charge of the program. It also reminded me of the channeled information from Kryon, whose mission was to realign the magnetic grids of the Earth. According to an interview on PLANETLightworker.com, with Lee Carroll, who channels Kryon; Kryon and his entourage completed their work on the magnetic grid system in 2002. Carroll says in the interview, "There is much physical evidence to support this. The magnetic grids have shifted more in the last ten years than in the preceding ninety. The Jeppeson map company in Denver, Colorado, for example, is busy remaking air maps and runways are being renumbered."

The GG went on to say that they felt our watchers would soon make themselves known to the general public:

> *"We feel that in the very near future beings from the Pleiades will be making themselves widely known and that will portend a significant change in how the inhabitants of the planet Earth view themselves and how they treat the planet. The Pleiades' contingent will caution us with tales of the damage they did to their own home world by raping the planet of its resources and giving nothing back. Once these beings make themselves known to all, they will continue to instruct us with regard to alternate fuels and methods that will enable us to get back on track with regard to caring for our planet."*

I had a book in my library that I bought and never got around to reading, but after this section was dictated, I pulled it out. The book is called "Pleiadian Perspectives on Human Evolution" and it was channeled/written by Amorah Quan Yi, a healer and psychic. I randomly opened the book to the Introduction, and two phrases popped off the page at me: The author refers to the "Pleiadian Emissaries of Light" and notes that the Earth is a "cosmic stepping stone." I plan to read this book as soon as I have a little time, but it's immediately intriguing to me that the Pleiadians are associated in this book with the light, just as the GG associates them with the light. I don't know what is meant by the Earth being a cosmic stepping stone, but that could explain why we have watchers to make sure we don't blow it up.

The GG also mentioned a contingent from Arcturus, and while looking for information about them, I found a book called, "We The Arcturians," that was channeled/written by Dr. Norma J. Milanovich with Betty Rice and Cynthia Ploski. This book details the Arcturian culture and their mission on the planet Earth. Here's a short excerpt:

> "...they [the Arcturians] are here to assist the Earth as it enters a new age of spirituality. They cannot interfere with the decision-making process of any Earthling. They are here to educate us and to help us raise the vibrations of all who choose to journey to the level of the new dimension that we are about to enter."

This book was first printed in 1990, and the information is consistent with what the GG dictated to me in mid-2008. I've always believed in life on other planets, it doesn't make sense to me that only our planet is inhabited by life forms. I hope they ARE friendly and that I'm still incarnated here when they do make themselves known!

During the late 80s and early 90s, I read every book that was written about alien abductions—the subject fascinated me as much as it scared the pantyhose off of me! To be dragged out of bed, taken to a space ship, and experimented on? What a horrible thing to endure. Too many people reported the experience for it to not be true—this is one of those things that people are not going to make up to draw attention to themselves—no one wants that kind of attention. So I was very glad that the GG continued their discussion about extraterrestrials by addressing this subject.

"Participation in an human/alien breeding program was the price for advanced technology and this was the deal that was made with the highest level of government officials throughout the planet Earth. This contract was made with the Zeta Reticuli, who were facing extinction. They destroyed their worlds and their race would have died out if not for this program. They wished to re-seed their planet using a combination of human and Zeta DNA. This is not a foreign concept in the Universe as the planet Earth was originally seeded with alien DNA.

The abductions and experiments are basically over as the new being is ready to seed not only the Zeta Reticuli's planets, but to re-seed the planet Earth should it ever become necessary. Something for you to know and remember is that superior technology does not mean superior common sense. Just because beings are from other planets does not mean they do not make mistakes! As we become more aware of them we need to understand that we are the ones in charge of our planet and others are here as our watchers and advisors.

Something important that people need to know is that only people who agreed to participate were taken and included in the genetic program. Because of the veil, many do not remember that this was part of their contract. It is important to note that even though care was taken to erase memories to avoid trauma, the extreme trauma of being taken caused many participants to experience mental anguish and great fear, although they didn't understand why. This was unfortunate and was not meant to happen.

Families were often chosen for this work, since it was a genetic study, and that is why you hear about multiple abductions within families. Some participants recognized that they were part of something great and wonderful and important for the universal good. Others could not get past their fear and efforts to work with them and make them forget sometimes did not work. Our understanding is that this program has ceased, but there is still on-going contact between parents and their universal children."

There is a television show "Alien Abductions—True Confessions," on WE TV, where women tell the stories, in great detail, of their alien abductions. It is heartbreaking and fascinating to hear how these experiences affected their lives and to see the differences in the way each woman looks at her personal experience. The best part of this show, other than how brave these women are to step forward with their stories to help others who went through or are going through a similar experience, is when they interview friends and family members of the abductee. Their friends and family believe the abductee is telling the truth, and they are going on national television and saying so—opening themselves for almost as much ridicule as the abductee. I read in the newspaper recently about a poll where 50% of those polled said they believe in aliens. Are this many people crazy?

And with the thought of people thinking that I'm crazy weighing heavily on my mind, I very much wanted to consider this next section to be of a purely personal nature and not include it in this book. But the GG insisted that I go forward with it, and so I get another opportunity to push aside my fear and share with all of you something that I would not even choose to share with my own family members or my best friends.

"Sherri, it is time to speak of your association with extraterrestrials. There is an experience that you had when you were 5 years old that you remember and still think about to this day. What you recall is one of several visitations that you have had during this lifetime, all of which took place when you were a baby and a small child. These visitations stopped when you were 12 years old. Beings from the Pleides visited you and talked with you to help you adjust to your surroundings. You do not remember talking with ETs. What you recall is little animal playmates that you decided lived under your bed. Most of the visitations took place before your first birthday and between your fourth and fifth birthdays."

I have no recollections whatsoever of ever being visited by aliens or abducted by aliens. I can recall reading Budd Hopkins' and Whitley Streiber's books and being absolutely terrified. Every time I read one, I would think to myself, "Thank God, this is not happening to me!" I cannot begin to imagine the fear of waking up, unable to move, and seeing ETs surrounding your bed, regardless of whether or not you contracted for it. What I do recall, though, are mice. Yes, mice. I used to think that I had talking mice as playmates and they lived under my bed. I thought this was my version of an invisible friend. I remember having make-believe mice as playmates when I was around 5 years old, but I don't remember anything else about it.

"After you were born, it was becoming clear that the incarnation you signed up for was not the one

145

you were going to get. Things were changing around you, and when you were a baby, you very much wanted to leave the body and begin anew. Adjustments were made to de-sensitize you so that you could remain where you were and accumulate the experiences that you needed to accumulate. Changes were taking place that were making it increasingly difficult for you to have the life experiences that were planned, and you recognized this on a subconscious level. You came into this incarnation with great sensitivity and empathy towards humankind, animalkind and plantlife, and the family you were in was changing and no longer the best possible fit. There were issues when you were a small baby that caused you to nearly end the incarnation. These issues were surrounding the entity who plays the role of your father in this incarnation. Changes within him severely affected the atmosphere of the home and you felt that you simply could not accomplish what you needed to accomplish if you stayed. But so many things were put into place and planned that this incarnation had to march on. You could not simply pull the plug and start anew because the timing would not be right again. You needed to be in certain places at certain times to fulfill contracts that were made. You had to stay and therefore, an emergency medical team, so to speak, made regular contact with you to work with you and counsel you so you could continue with your life plan. This was accomplished by taking you to the ship at night while you slept. As a baby, and as a small child, you were still awake enough to not be frightened, but pictures were

146

given to you to cover the experience, thus the mice who lived under the bed were born. You are not the only person this happened to. There are many, many entities currently incarnated who found themselves in need of an emergency readjustment due to circumstances changing or the entity feeling that the circumstances were not as ideal as they originally thought they would be. In fact, readjusting the energies up and down are things that happen quite often to people as they sleep at night. Because of free will, things change and then adjustments must be made to make sure that the mission can continue. Do you understand what we are saying to you?"

I certainly understood it on an "hmmm" level. I definitely remember mice that seemed quite real to me at the time, but nothing beyond that, so it's hard for me to comment on this information. It certainly sounds plausible that circumstances could change due to free will, and an entity might want to change his circumstances. I also know from what the GG dictated about suicide and murder, that when someone's life ends sooner than planned, there is a lot of scurrying to create new windows of opportunity for everyone involved, and it can be very far-reaching. So it makes sense that there would be universal EMTs ready to help in these types of situations. I do recall my Mother telling me that I contracted pneumonia and was very sick when I was a small baby, I think around 3 months old. At the very least, this information from the GG makes for a very interesting story and might make us think twice before discounting kids who have invisible friends or animals for "playmates!"

The GG continued dictating information that was connected to ETs for several days. Because much of this information also has to do with the changes taking place on our planet, I wasn't sure where it should fit into this book. In the end, I opted to include it all in this chapter because of the ET connection, even though you'll see that it's about much more than visitors to our planet.

> *"A global outlook is crucial at this point in the Earth's transition. It is one of the things that will help bring in more light and make the transition easier on all who are incarnated, and on the Earth herself. A global outlook is nothing more than allowing for the fact that all human beings have rights and the number one right is free will. All on this planet revolves around free will. It is the reason for incarnations here—to see if with free will entities can remember their path and stay on their path. Free will coupled with the lower vibrations on the planet make it difficult for human beings to stay on the path. This is the great test. The planet is about to change and will begin to take a global viewpoint rather than feeling that their country is the only one that counts. These wars have all been fought on the basis of religion, but religion is not what inspired them— it was commerce and business and wealth, and most of all, power that inspires war. War and the possibility of great global catastrophe is one reason so many entities who are whole in the light have been incarnated on this planet, and are also surrounding it at the present time. As the time approaches for the shift, you will see a complete breakdown in the religious belief systems that are so important to many people at the present time. When people stop segregating themselves into religious groups and start looking at mankind as a whole, we will have made great progress on planet Earth and we will see the light burning*

148

much more brightly. We are not saying that people should not be spiritual, we are saying that people should be concerned about other people no matter what religion or nationality they might be. The United States needs to take the lead. Yes, it is true that there are terrorist groups and terrorist cells, but the United States of America can help this planet make much progress if the country will wake up to the knowledge that there are many cultures and ways of life that are just as important, if not more important, than the United States. That is when true progress is made."

At this point, I questioned the GG about pinpointing the United States.

"You are concerned that we continue to speak of the United States rather than other parts of the globe. That is because the bulk of the Atlanteans are in the United States. The United States is the new Atlantis, and because the actions and attitudes of these reincarnated Atlanteans is so important to the outcome of this great experiment we tend to focus our attention here. This time is all about coming together as one world and soon things will happen that will force this to come about. One of the major things that will happen is that there will be more sightings of so-called UFOs than ever before, and the difference is that there will be sightings by large groups of people who will be believed. There will be so many sightings that the government will not be able to subdue them. People will learn that they are not alone in the universe. This knowledge will cause countries to come together as a united planet with

a united cause. The ETs will help the planet understand that there is more, so much more, than we have been allowed to know. The unbridled knowledge that there is life outside of our own planet is going to be a large turning point, and it is very close at hand."

From a personal point of view, I am intrigued that I have no problem whatsoever believing in ETs, believing they have visited Earth, and are visiting now. But I find it disconcerting, to say the least, to think that an ET Emergency Medical Team treated me as a child and made me think they were little mice friends! And if waking up one day and seeing a big 'ol flying saucer up in the sky is the kick in the butt we need to start thinking globally, I hope we see it soon!

The GG concluded their dictation about extraterrestrials with the following:

"World governments are very much aware of the on-going presence of those from other planets here on Earth, but they choose to cloak it all in secrecy believing that people cannot accept the truth of it. They are wrong, as many believe and want to know the truth, and the truth of it will come out eventually as more and more people share their contact experiences. It will come out that we are sharing our universe, and indeed our planet, with those who originated on other planets. In fact, many of the souls incarnated here on the planet Earth originated on other planets. It is not unusual for souls to have incarnations on different planets to pursue different courses of learning. Not every planet is the schoolhouse that the Earth is—the Earth is one of the most difficult classrooms in which to

150

grow and learn. There are many lessons to be learned and many ways to learn them, and sometimes the environment of one planet is a better fit than another for the intended curriculum. It's not a usual practice for most souls on Earth, but it is not uncommon among lightworkers."

CHAPTER EIGHT
MEDITATION

"The act of meditating will enable us to open our minds, to still the mind so that we listen within and hear what is being said to us. We can listen and our heads will be filled with the things you (Sherri) call 'word bubbles,' where complete thoughts spring to the forefront of your mind as fully developed ideas for you to run with! This is a form of connection to the Source, but it only touches the barest surface of what is possible.

To connect with the Source, you must go deeper, and for that to happen there must be discipline to meditate at the same time each and every day and to give it the time and care that it needs. For goodness sake, Sherri, if people knew they would experience joy and happiness by giving up a lousy fifteen to thirty minutes a day why would they not do so? Does it make any sense to you? It's because they are asleep and must be awakened.

So how do we awaken the masses? That's the hard part, my dear! Lightworkers do it by setting an example, by living what they believe. Each life touches other lives and those they touch, touch even more lives, and so on and on. One single life will ultimately touch countless other lives. People see someone who is joyful and happy and everything seems to be going so well for that person. They ask that person how it is, why it is that way for them? Because they are asking, instead of being preached to, they are more apt to listen!"

153

I've been meditating since the 80s, and have found it to be calming *and* a great way to connect to the universal consciousness. Often at work, people ask me how I come up with so many ideas, and the answer is that I don't come up with them at all, I let them come to me. By meditating you can connect to the universal consciousness and ideas will flow to you. I meditate in two ways, the first is a more formal meditation where I clear my mind and try to keep it clear; and the second is just by sitting quietly in a room by myself with no TV, no radio, and no books and *listening* to whatever pops into my head. There are also many guided meditations available—I highly recommend Doreen Virtue's guided meditations to help us get in touch with our guardian angels, and Shirley MacLaine's meditation CDs.

I clearly remember sitting in Tony's Restaurant in Middletown, New York, with my friend, Jean Van Anglen. She was telling me about a new book called "Out on a Limb" by Shirley MacLaine. She was very excited about the book, and loaned me her copy. After I read it, I went out and bought my own copy and I have it still, along with every book Ms. MacLaine has ever written! I was at the beginning of my search for truth and enlightenment, and Shirley was doing all the work and sharing it with the world through her books. Every book she wrote took me further along my path and prompted me to learn more about the subjects she wrote about. I learned a lot about meditation and reincarnation from her books and tapes, and I cringe every time I hear a joke made about her on TV. Shirley MacLaine put herself on the front line and she's no doubt paid the price for it. She was fearless years ago when she wrote "Out on a Limb" and she's still fearless with her newest book, "Sage-ing while Age-ing." I was once asked who I would have dinner with if I could have dinner with anyone in the world. I didn't have to think long to come up with an answer—Shirley MacLaine, of course! I've never met her, but if it weren't for Shirley MacLaine, I doubt that I would have had the guts to write this book—and let's face it, I didn't break any records rushing to get it published!

Back to meditation! Meditating has helped me in so many ways, and on so many levels. I believe it helps me maintain my mental and physical health and well being! How? Things always seem easier to deal with at work and at home after 15 minutes of meditation, and I believe many studies have been done that prove it helps lower blood pressure. I know that meditating helped me open my mind enough to begin automatic writing. Meditation is not hard and it's something that everyone can do—it just takes patience and a little bit of a time commitment. If you wiggle around a lot and can't sit still at first, so what? Practice makes perfect, and you'll get better and better at it every day. Here are some simple, basic steps to help you get started.

<u>Basic instructions to begin meditating</u>

- Pick a time of day when you can sit in undisturbed silence for at least 15-20 minutes.
- Try to meditate at the same time each day.
- Sit upright in a comfortable chair.
- If you want to burn a candle and/or incense, go ahead.
- Close your eyes and start to clear your mind.
- As thoughts come in, don't worry about it, just acknowledge them and send them away. You can think about those things later!
- Sit quietly for 15 – 20 minutes—set a timer if you want to.
- When you're finished meditating, don't forget to blow out candles and incense if you used them!

The more you meditate, the easier it will become!

CHAPTER NINE
Automatic Writing

Sometime in 1987 or 1988, I was in a book store and I noticed a display of books by the cash register. They were all titles by Ruth Montgomery and the first two that caught my eye were, "A Search for the Truth," and "Aliens Among Us." I bought them immediately and read them both back-to-back in record time. I was at the beginning of my own search for the truth, and I don't think it was a coincidence that I decided to go to the mall that night!

Everyone has role models, and when I was young, Mary Tyler Moore and Marlo Thomas were at the top of my list. They were on the front line by taking the roles of women who pursued careers instead of marriage—their characters made their own choices and supported themselves—their TV shows were ground-breaking and a great inspiration to me and to many young women. As soon as I read "A Search for the Truth," Ruth Montgomery went to the top of my list.

Here was a woman with a fabulous career, who was very much in the public eye, and who risked her reputation by revealing to the world that she communicated with the spirit world through automatic writing. I instinctively knew that no one would risk their reputation in this way if they weren't on a very important mission. Let me share a little bit of Ruth's background with you. She was a reporter for such newspapers as the Chicago Tribune and the New York Daily News, before moving to Washington, D.C., where she became a correspondent for the International News Service in the 1950s. She traveled the world as a foreign correspondent and won several journalism awards. It seemed to me that she had everything to lose and nothing to gain by writing these books.

In 1958, she met a medium named Arthur Ford, who told her that she could do automatic writing. An entity named "Lily" wrote with her, and when Arthur Ford passed over, he also participated in dictating information to Ms. Montgomery. All told, I believe the information she received was enough to fill 12 books!

The more Ruth Montgomery books I read, the more I wanted to communicate with the other side, too. I tried for several months and nothing happened, until that amazing night that my Guide, Jeremy, first came through during a psychic development class I was attending. When Cyndi (the psychic in Monticello I mentioned at the beginning of this book) said, "We're going to practice automatic writing tonight," I said I couldn't do it. As the words were coming out of my mouth, "someone" (Jeremy) gripped my hand and started drawing circles. I couldn't believe it! The entire class was watching me and I was watching my hand move by itself! I learned to control it, and started a wonderful relationship writing every day with Jeremy and other Guides and entities that dropped in to impart information and wisdom.

I said it in the beginning of this book, and I'm going to say it again now; there is nothing special about my ability to do automatic writing. Anyone who wants to do it can do it. Anyone who wants to be in touch with their guides, their guardian angels, and even the Archangels can do it—you just have talk to them, they will hear you. And if you open your mind, you will sense "word bubbles in your head" or maybe you will see pictures in your mind—you can establish an on-going communication with your guides and angels. You can communicate one way or several ways—just be open and you'll find the way or ways that are right for you. Long before I started automatic writing, I would receive "word bubbles" in my head—fully formed thoughts that were full of wisdom or great ideas. I started paying more and more attention to them and I noticed that most of these communications came to me when I was in the shower or commuting to or from work. In other words, when I was *alone*! When I shared this with Cyndi, she told me that it was Jeremy, my guide, communicating with me. The first thing I said upon hearing this was, "What! He's seeing me naked?" Never mind the awe and thrill of spiritual communication! All I was concerned about was being seen in the shower! For the record, Cyndi said that spirits don't see us as bodies, they see our light, our spirit, our aura—so don't worry about receiving word bubbles in the shower! My point here is that YOU CAN COMMUNICATE if you want to! It might not happen on your timetable (remember, I didn't think it would happen for me, either!) but if you stick with it, it will happen. If you'd like to communicate via automatic writing, here's how I do it:

- Choose a time of day when you can sit undisturbed for at least 15 minutes.
- Sit comfortably with a pad of paper on the table in front of you and hold a pen or pencil loosely in your hand with the tip of your writing instrument touching the paper. You can use a computer keyboard instead of pad and paper.
- Say a prayer of protection; here's mine (Cyndi gave this to me in 1987): "I am protected by the love of God, only those entities of the highest intentions can pass through my door. If others should try, my door will immediately close, effectively blocking them out. This is my prayer of protection. Amen."
- Write on the top of the paper, "Will someone write with me?"
- Clear your mind and wait. If it helps you to burn incense or candles, go right ahead. Don't forget to blow them out when you're finished.
- If nothing happens within the first five minutes, end the session, it won't be happening that day.
- Keep trying again until you make contact!

Your first connection:

- When you first connect, it will feel like someone is grasping your hand and/or your arm. Just relax—let it happen.

- You will most likely experience circles, figure 8s, and back and forth movements with your pen or pencil.

- Ask the entity for his or her name and ask the entity what his or her relationship is to you. Don't go any further until you start to write words and you know who you're writing with.

- Next, ask the entity for a message; i.e., "Do you have something to share with me?" Write this down on the paper and wait for a response. As you get information, you can ask questions about what you're receiving—just write them down (or type them) and wait for the response.

- When you and/or your guide(s) are finished, you'll feel the pen (or your hands if your typing) relax. Be sure to thank your guide(s) for working with you. After I say, "Thank you," or when my guides are finished, they generally write, "Go in Peace," to signify the end of a session. You'll establish a similar type of routine with your guide(s).

Continued sessions:

Always do your automatic writing at the same time each day. Just because an entity doesn't happen to be in a body, doesn't mean that he or she doesn't have things to do! Be respectful of your guide(s') time. If you can't make a session, tell your guide(s) you aren't coming that day. You can use paper and pen or your computer keyboard; ALWAYS say a prayer of protection before each session.

160

Please don't become discouraged like I did when it didn't happen for me right away. With a little time and practice, you'll be taking dictation from your Guides and I'll be reading *your* book!

CHAPTER TEN
"Knowing doesn't make it easier"

While working on this book, two tragedies happened in my family—first my beautiful sister-in-law, Denise Bland, died suddenly and tragically at the heartbreaking age of just 46 years old. Then my beloved Mother, Marjorie Knapp Ihburg, just 68 years old, lost a 16-month battle with brain cancer. Several years ago, one of my favorite cousins, Linda Knapp (who was part of the GG for this book) died in a tragic car accident on Christmas Eve, leaving behind two small children and her fiancé—she was 40 years old. I loved all three of these women very much and my heart was broken when they left what I felt to be "early."

The loss of my Mother in June 2008 was the worse experience of my life so far. She was very strong, had beaten lung cancer and it really looked like the brain cancer was in remission. On May 1, 2008, we got the news that her doctor discovered new brain lesions, and said she couldn't have any more radiation treatments. The entire family was in shock and there was nothing that could be done—it was just a matter of time. I immediately flew to New York to see her, and she flew to Orlando the following week for our first official family reunion. That reunion was planned for a year in advance and I'm so glad we decided to do it—we didn't know at the time we were planning it that it would be Mom's opportunity to see her family together for the last time. At first my Mother's Sister, and my Aunt, Sandra Knapp, flew from Florida to New York to take care of her so she could remain at home, and then both of my sisters took leaves from their jobs and moved into Mom's house, too, to take care of her—all three of them are truly angels on Earth, as are all care-givers.

I got a call on June 23rd with the news that she had about a week left, and I immediately started making plans to fly home.

A half hour later I got another call that she had passed over to the other side. I was happy that she was released from all the pain—but I am heartbroken to have lost her so early and in such an awful way. I doubt that I will ever stop missing her.

Speaking for myself, having the knowledge that we plan our lives and that accidents are *windows of opportunity* for us to learn and grow *did not* stop the pain I felt and still feel at the loss of my Cousin, my Sister-in-Law, and my Mother. In fact as I'm writing this now I have tears streaming down my face. All three created many windows of opportunity for many people with their "early" exits from this plane of existence, and through their sacrifice. And through my tears, I am thankful for the ways they made this incarnation more joyful, and I'm thankful to them for the opportunities they provided for their loved ones to learn and to grow.

If I've learned nothing else from taking the dictation and organizing the material for this book, I've learned that being incarnated and living our lives means that we are going to have both heart-breaking and difficult situations, experiences that will cause us pain. And sometimes it will seem like that pain is too much to bear. I've learned that it's how we deal with these experiences that makes *all the difference* in how successful we are in reaching our goals for each incarnation.

Writing this book has taught me to look for life scripts in my own life and to own up to the ones I discovered through these writings. There was a time in my life that I would never have believed or accepted the fact that I would do anything to stagnate my growth, and I've learned that nothing was further from the truth!

I've learned a great deal from the information channeled to me by the GG and I'm so grateful to them for taking the time to give me this information, and more importantly for pushing me to put it all into book form. The writing of this book has been an eye-opening and painful growth experience for me. I had to overcome a very great fear of being labeled a "weirdo" for coming out of the closet and admitting that I meditate, that I believe in reincarnation and aliens from other planets, and that I receive messages from those on the other side of the veil. By coming out of the closet and finally writing this book after years of trying to avoid it, I learned to recognize life scripts and to make the changes necessary to learn, grow, and accomplish my goals for this lifetime. I'm learning to work through the pain of life-changing accidents. Helping people to let go of fear, make some sense out of our lives, and learning to move forward with our lives—that is the purpose of this book. I remember a billboard that was up for awhile on Sand Lake Road near my home in Orlando—the headline said, "The Story of You." I know it was an advertisement for a newspaper, but that phrase has become my new mantra. It really sums up what this book is all about—each one of us is writing our life story, each day is another chapter and we each have the power to make our individual story, our current lifetime, the great success we planned for ourselves when we penned the outline at the planning table with our loved ones.

About the Author

In the late 1980's, during a psychic development class in upstate New York. Sherri made "first contact" with her Spirit Guides through Automatic Writing. In 2005, several of her Guides formed a group to dictate the information and wisdom that formed the basis for Sherri's book, "Windows of Opportunity." During the Conference, Sherri will introduce two important concepts from the book, "Relationship Villains" and "Windows of Opportunity," and discuss their connection to accelerated Spiritual Growth.

Sherri is the Director of Specialty Sales for a large vacation resort in Orlando, Florida, and holds degrees in English and Communications. In the early 90's, Sherri studied Herbology with Rosemary Gladstar, and went on to earn a Doctor of Naturopathy degree from the Clayton College of Natural Health in 1998.

"Windows of Opportunity," due out this Summer from Ozark Mountain Publishing, is Sherri's first published book. She is currently working with her Guide Group on her second manuscript, tentatively titled, "Raising your Vibrations for the New Age."

Other Books Published
by
Ozark Mountain Publishing, Inc.

Continue for more books by Ozark Mountain Publishing, Inc.

For more information about any of the above titles, soon to be released titles, or other items in our catalog, write or visit our website:

OZARK
MOUNTAIN
PUBLISHING

PO Box 754
Huntsville, AR 72740
www.ozarkmt.com
1-800-935-0045/479-738-2348
Wholesale Inquiries Welcome